CRGC

THE
UNTOLD
STORY

Praise for Raj Kanwar

'A smooth, well-oiled read both for the professional and the uninitiated – here's the story of the early days of India's quest for oil and natural gas. Seasoned veteran Raj Kanwar brings alive the pioneers who opened the doors and made it possible. An excellent read...'
– Ganesh Saili

'Raj Kanwar is a noted writer and journalist of Dehra Dun, with many years of experience. He has been closely associated with ONGC for much of his life, and this book represents part of his vast knowledge on the organisation.'

– Roshen Dalal

A man who will ride his bicycle up the drive at Teen Murti Marg to call on the occupant and two minutes later ride out again in the back seat of the Prime Minister's car, his pen scratching furiously as Nehru holds forth on the way to the airport, will go far. Sixty years later, Raj Kanwar is still on the road, a chancer who deserves all our admiration.
– Irwin Allan Sealy

Raj Kanwar, the scribe and chronicler of the Doon Valley down the decades now turns his prolific pen towards the narration of the story of the Oil and Natural Gas Commission (ONGC) which he has known as an insider from its nascent days. Written in an appealing vein, the history of this premier Public Sector undertaking will appeal to the general reader and those interested in technological details alike. Hitherto unknown facts about the Oil Industry in general and the ONGC in particular come to light as one reads on. It has the genre of a thriller at many places.

– Arvindar Singh

ONGC
THE UNTOLD STORY

RAJ KANWAR

B L O O M S B U R Y
NEW DELHI • LONDON • OXFORD • NEW YORK • SYDNEY

BLOOMSBURY INDIA
Bloomsbury Publishing India Pvt. Ltd
Second Floor, LSC Building No. 4, DDA Complex, Pocket C – 6 & 7,
Vasant Kunj, New Delhi 110070

BLOOMSBURY, BLOOMSBURY PRIME and the Diana logo are trademarks of
Bloomsbury Publishing Plc

First published 2019

ISBN: 978-93-88271-39-4

2 4 6 8 10 9 7 5 3

Printed and bound in India by Rajkamal Electric Press, Kundli, Haryana.

Bloomsbury Publishing Plc makes every effort to ensure that the papers used in
the manufacture of our books are natural, recyclable products made from wood
grown in well-managed forests. Our manufacturing processes conform to the
environmental regulations of the country of origin

To find out more about our authors and books visit www.bloomsbury.com
and sign up for our newsletters

Dedicated to

My wife Amber, daughter Minnie, sons Manav and Gagan, and grandchildren Ambika, Kaveri, Kiara and Vir

Contents

Chairmen and Managing Directors

The Incumbent Chairman and Managing Director

PART II
KDMIPE: A Jewel in ONGC's Crown

Men Behind KDMIPE

EPILOGUE

DR. K. K. PAUL
Governor, Uttarakhand

सत्यमेव जयते

RAJ BHAWAN
DEHRADUN-248003
1 June 2018

FOREWORD

Located in the heart of the picturesque Doon Valley, Dehra Dun of yesteryears used to be an idyllic and sleepy town. Its first major expansion happened only after Independence, when a large number of Punjabis and other migrants made the town their home. Economic boom had not by then hit the town. The common means of commuting were bicycles and tongas.

There were then no viable commercial activities in the town; as a result, most of the young people migrated in search of greener pastures. It was the situation that then prevailed in Dehra Dun. The town underwent a sea change in 1956 when ONGC established its headquarters here. The unemployed youth found employment and idle businesses received a boost. Dehra Dun soon began to taste the fruits of an economic boom and shortly after, this sleepy town turned into a flourishing city.

I understand that as a young journalist, in the mid 1950s, Raj Kanwar had been in regular contact with the then Minister of State for Mines and Oil, Shri KD Malaviya. At the latter's behest, he joined the ONGC as its first Public Relations Officer. Though he was in the ONGC barely for three years, yet he had made substantial contacts that came handy later. In 2004, Kanwar was commissioned to write the history of ONGC that was formally released in 2006.

I have known Raj ever since I came to Dehra Dun and have read with admiration his articles on a variety of subjects.

I am happy to learn that he has now once again chosen to write about some hitherto unknown facts of ONGC including how and why Dehra Dun came to become the headquarters of ONGC—a company of national importance.

I am sure that the book will be extremely readable with anecdotes of historical value. I wish him Godspeed.

(Dr. K.K. Paul)

ACKNOWLEDGEMENTS

I am in deep gratitude to my wife Amber, daughter Minnie and sons Manav and Gagan who have been consistently imploring me to write a book on any subject of my choice. Their logic was that articles for newspapers and magazines have a short shelf life; a book, on the other hand, will be my literary legacy. Bowing to their pressing entreaty, I decided to write first about ONGC – a subject that is very dear to my heart; the second book, God willing, will be on the multifaceted city of Dehra Dun that has now been my *karambhoomi* for the past seven decades.

I am grateful to Uttarakhand Governor Dr. KK Paul who encouraged me, and was kind enough to write its Foreword. I am also greatly indebted to Bikash Chandra Bora, C&MD of both Oil India Ltd and ONGC at different times, for giving me from time to time his advice. LL Bhandari, former chairman and managing director, too gave me not only invaluable inputs but also some rare photographs from his family albums.

Likewise ONGC veterans, Baldev Singh and Krishan Kumar provided me with important inputs and photographs. Also greatly helpful were Chris (son of Leslie James Johnson) and Shuva (daughter of Subir Raha) who readily sent me invaluable photographs from their respective family archives.

Here, I must acknowledge that much of the information in the Prologue about how, when and where crude oil was first discovered in the world is based on *The Prize* the celebrated book by Daniel Yergin.

I also must put on record my appreciation of the guidance that the BP's New Delhi-based Director Corporate Communications, Narayani Mahil has been giving to me from time to time.

I must thank my literary agent Ms. Dipti Patel who brought Bloomsbury on the table as the publishers. My thanks are also due to my friend Anil Maheshwari, a Delhi-based author and journalist, for his timely guidance.

Last but not least I must acknowledge the significant contribution made by my secretary Amit Sharma who untiringly spent hours in directly typing from my dictation the entire manuscript.

And finally, I am grateful to my guardian angel for keeping me in good health and spirits that helped me work virtually eight hours a day.

INTRODUCTION

Over the past 60 plus years, ONGC and I seem to have developed inextricable and somewhat unusual ties, more like an umbilical cord. Dehra Dun is the common denominator in this relationship. Like any entity, ONGC had made a humble beginning. And in no time, it had found its bearings and started growing at a rapid pace. Starting with barely 60 employees in 1956, ONGC today has 33,000 staffers on its roll. It is now one of the most profitable public sector oil companies in the country. In the year 2016-17, it made a gigantic profit of ₹17,900 crore.

Now a brief narrative about how I first came in contact with the founding father of ONGC, KD Malaviya, and its young pioneers! That in itself is an interesting story and has been amply written about in the pages that follow.

It was those early contacts that created some sort of emotional empathy between me and ONGCians. In retrospect, it appears that I was destined to become an integral part of ONGC that was then growing by leaps and bounds.

With my rich and varied background in journalism and public relations, Malaviya did not think twice in appointing me as ONGC's first public relations officer, and posting me at Baroda. From Baroda to *Sibsagar* in Assam was a long way both physically and metaphorically. The most important event during my tenure in Assam was the Chinese aggression of October-November 1962.

I had already served three years in ONGC and the very prospect of spending the rest of my life in a public sector company appeared daunting. Having been an independent journalist much of my young life, I did not relish the file-pushing tedium that is an integral part of bureaucratic routine. I took leave from ONGC and stopped in Calcutta en route for a few days.

That brief stay in Calcutta was to change my professional trajectory. A job was offered to me by Harbans Lal Malhotra & Sons – the then blades kings of India – to set up their public relations and advertising department that I readily accepted. However, the façade of Calcutta life soon faded. I yearned to return to the Valley that was green, even 55 years ago. My home beckoned me, though there was no "home" in the real sense. My father had passed away in August 1962.

My return to Dehra Dun was eventful. I launched '*Witness*' – *a newsweekly with a difference* – in August 1964. It became an instant hit. I also resumed with vengeance my contacts with ONGC and its officials. *Witness* extensively covered ONGC and other Dehra Dun-based government departments such like the Survey of India, Forest Research Institute et al. I also got married in 1965. SK Oilfield Equipment Co Pvt Ltd made its bow in 1970. Slowly but surely, SK Oilfield started growing and set up its offices in Bombay, Sibsagar and Delhi. I retired as its chairman in 2000 when I turned 70. In 2004, Subir Raha, the then ONGC's C&MD commissioned me to write its history of 50 years. The book was released on 14 August 2006 under the title *Upstream India*.

DURING the past 18 years, I must have written over 1500 articles on a wide variety of subjects. Fortuitously, a large number of these articles cover the numerous facets of ONGC that had over the years become my pet subject. Not many people, not even ONGCians, know about the early days of ONGC. How and when it was born and what were its teething troubles and growing pains?

It is this awareness that has motivated me to publish an anthology of some of my articles on ONGC. This then is the rationale behind *The Untold Story*.

PART I

ONGC
THE
UNTOLD
STORY

PROLOGUE

How, when and where crude oil was first discovered in the world should make for fascinating reading. Even though the men who found the oil were ordinary men yet their obsession with performing exceptional feats or making stunning discoveries or amazing inventions turned them into extraordinary men.

These men were George Bissell and Edwin Drake whose names will always live so long the oil industry exists.

However, the discovery of oil in the middle of the nineteenth century was just a happenstance. According to Daniel Yergin, its genesis lay in a 'series of accidental glimpses'. In his magnum opus, *The Prize*, Yergin credits George Bissell of Titusville, Pennsylvania for discovering oil and laying the foundation of the oil industry as it is known today.

George Bissell was essentially a self-taught and self-made man. In mid 1850s, when law and order, as it is known today, was conspicuously absent, the young Bissell lived on his wits and guts. He took tuitions and wrote articles to pay for his college education. For a while, he taught Latin and Greek too. He also worked as a journalist in Washington DC and later became the principal of a high school in New Orleans.

Col Edwin Drake (in top hat) at the first ever drilled oil
well in Titusville, Pennsylvania in 1859.
Courtesy: Daniel Yergin

George Bissell –
considered as the
Father of Oil Industry.
Courtesy: Daniel Yergin

His quest for knowledge did not have any limits; he had a knack for learning languages, and at one time he acquired fluency in Portuguese, Spanish, French, Hebrew, and learned to read and write Latin, modern Greek as also Sanskrit.

Unfortunately, on his homeward journey, he fell ill. It was one of those coincidences when Bissell encountered people gathering in a primitive way something akin to '*rock oil*' that was then used as folk medicine for a variety of ailments. A string of coincidences followed in the next few months. Shrewd and highly educated as he was, Bissell soon realized that this '*rock oil*' could easily be used as an illuminant for lighting lamps. He visualized he could become rich by exploring and exploiting this rare commodity. Then for the following six years, Bissell dreamt, drank and ate this oil; so obsessive he had become.

To cut the long story short, Bissell managed to put together a group of investors in 1854, and engaged one Prof. Benjamin Silliman of Yale University to analyze the numerous properties of 'rock oil' just to confirm whether it could be used both as an illuminant and lubricant.

There were several problems with Silliman but finally the group of investors headed by Bissell was able to get a very optimistic report from the professor. Yergin further says in *The Prize*, *'Silliman's study was nothing less than a "turning point" in the establishment of petroleum business. Silliman banished any doubts about the potential new uses for 'rock oil'. His main finding was that the 'rock oil' could be brought to various levels of boiling and thus distilled into several fractions, all composed of carbon and hydrogen'.* His confirmation that it could also be used as an illuminant was most reassuring.

"They could not have chosen a better man for this purpose. Heavyset and vigorous with a 'jolly good face', Silliman carried one of the greatest and most respected names in the nineteenth century science. The son of the founder of American chemistry, he himself was one of the most distinguished scientists of his time; he was also the author of leading textbooks on physics and chemistry", was Yergin's eloquent description of the professor who was destined to become the first ever scientist to undertake research in what was then called, 'rock oil'.

First Incorporated Oil Company

Professor Silliman's report helped Bissell and his group raise enough funds from some other investors; even the professor himself bought 200 shares, so confident was he about his own prognostication. A banker named James Townsend was also roped in. The new entity, Pennsylvania Rock Oil Company, thus became the first incorporated oil company in the world. And this assignment by Prof. Silliman became the first ever formal research conducted in respect of 'rock oil'.

The curiosity about the new illuminant and lubricant was confined only to the United States. Europe, long before this American enterprise, had become a small hub of an illuminant that later became known as kerosene. Since there were no professional scientists, everyone started using their own grey cells. A plumber and a pharmacist jointly developed the prototype of a lamp that could use kerosene.

Soon, kerosene became the new flavour of trade and commerce in Vienna. The kerosene business thrived so much that by 1860, about 150 villages mainly in Romania and Galicia produced 35,000 barrels of kerosene. What they did not have at that time was the know-how of drilling technology.

Search for a Drilling Tool

What Bissell and his fellow investors intended was to replicate the salt boring technique to rock oil. In other words, they wanted to find some tool or device that would drill rather than

dig for oil. By then no one had heard of a drilling rig or derrick. It was again by sheer coincidence or accident that Bissell came across pictures of several drilling derricks at a shop window. Instead of 'digging' for rock oil, as was then the practice, Bissell and his group decided to 'drill' for oil as they would drill for salt.

Enters 'Col' Edwin Drake...

It was at this stage that one Edwin Drake made his entry. He was a colourful character and jack of all trades and master of none. He had done multifarious jobs including that of a 'railroad conductor'. He was a great entertainer and storyteller and would often regale his little audience in a downtown hotel in New Haven with anecdotes and tall stories, born out of a fertile imagination.

By sheer chance, banker James Townsend also had his lodgings in the same hotel. Townsend took an instant liking to this loquacious man of 38 and often discussed with him about rock oil venture. It was easy for the banker to recruit this 'out-of-job' street-smart man. In order to confer some sort of respectability on his errand man, the banker called him 'Colonel'.

...and the Oil was Discovered

Thus decorated with the high sounding prefix of Colonel, Drake arrived in Titusville, a small village with a population of 150 in Pennsylvania. Most of its inhabitants were lumbermen in debt to the lumber store. A new enterprise called Seneca Oil Company was formed by the investors and Drake designated its general agent. The story in brief is that Drake eventually found oil after numerous disappointments, heartbreaks and paucity of funds; it was his determination that triumphed in the end and oil was discovered at 69 feet on a Saturday afternoon, 27 August 1859. That was the first oil discovery in the world in which a derrick-like structure was used.

Oil Scene Shifts to India

And several thousand miles away in India, around 1820s, another string of coincidences were occurring, in the dense forests, swamps and river beds in the extreme Northeastern corner of Assam.

One Lieutenant R. Wilcox of the 46th Regiment Native infantry was on a military mission there. What he accidentally encountered was great bubbling of gas and green petroleum. Later, many more military expeditions noticed identical signs of petroleum in its various hues from green to bluish-white and oil seepages. In 1865, HB Medlicott of Geological Survey of India accidentally also noticed much seepage while reporting on the coal-fields of upper Assam and recommended trial drilling in the area.

To once again cut the long story short, three wells were drilled in the Jaipur area that found some gas; however, there was very little oil. Simultaneously, on the recommendation of Medlicott, drilling was undertaken at the Makum- Namdang area on 26 March, 1867.

A scene from a rig site in Assam in 1860s.
Courtesy: Oil India Ltd

Oil was finally struck in the fourth well but its flow did not last long. Happily, the second attempt in the same area proved successful. Thus this second well at Makum became the first successful mechanically drilled well in Asia, just eight years after the Drake well.

Now on to ONGC

Why I dilated upon these early oil discoveries in the world was to underscore the point that oil was then discovered, by and large, just through sheer accident involving no exploration as it does today. From those early accidental and coincidental 'oil discoveries', the business of oil has today become dependent on highly sophisticated exploration sciences and state of the art tools. More importantly, the entire world has now become a borderless *single petroleum entity* in which multinational and national oil companies are exploring for oil away from their home bases and in far away, remote and at times virtually inaccessible regions.

CHAPTER 1

The Founding Father

KD Malaviya was undoubtedly the Father of India's national oil industry.

He was a gutsy leader and single handedly took up cudgels against the combined might of the multinational oil cartel and its influential supporters in the Indian government. His sustained effort led to the creation of a network of national oil companies in the country. He was a lone ranger who lived a dream and saw it fulfilled. The sobriquet, Father of Indian Oil Industry will always be his.

Keshava Deva Malaviya's life story has two fascinating, distinct chapters. The first chapter that began in 1929 was almost entirely devoted to the freedom struggle. He had by then obtained a degree in vegetable oil technology from Cawnpore's (now Kanpur) famed Harcourt Butler Institute of Technology and could have obtained a cushy job.  Instead, he plunged himself head **first** into the freedom movement. Between 1929 and 1942, Malaviya went to jail on nine different occasions. The last jail term was the longest and lasted from 1942 to 1946. Jawaharlal Nehru was his prison inmate during one of his incarcerations; the relationship that then grew between them was to play a historic role in the years to come in the creation of a national oil industry in the country.

The second chapter began in 1952 with his election to the first Lok Sabha that turned out to be the beginning of a new epoch in many ways. For Malaviya, the decade of 1950 was the most daunting and challenging. Nehru had made him a deputy minister in the Ministry of Natural Resources and Scientific Research, then headed by Maulana Abul Kalam Azad. Ironically, his portfolio at the Natural Resources division in the ministry did not include either petroleum or the Council of Scientific and Industrial Research (CSIR). It was possibly intended to be a rebuff to Malaviya.

Dr Shanti Swaroop Bhatnagar was then the secretary of that important department and his sway over the world of science and technology in India was then all-pervasive. He was in favour of permitting multinationals to look for the prospects of oil and gas in the country. Multinational companies such as Standard Oil Company (STANVAC) and Burmah Shell waited in the wings hoping to jump in at an opportune time that might come their way. Bhatnagar had almost decided to give a prospecting license to STANVAC in the Jaisalmer area of Rajasthan and a proposal to that effect had already been put up for Nehru's approval. Prospecting rights in Bengal and Assam had already gone to Burmah Shell that had been operating there for decades. It became a touch and go situation for Malaviya. To cut a long story short, Malaviya, with Nehru's help, managed to overcome these formidable hurdles, and finally laid a firm foundation for the formation of a national oil company. Thus, Oil and Natural Gas Commission made a modest beginning in 1956. Malaviya was already a minister and was a natural choice to be appointed its first chairman.

Jawaharlal Nehru's love and weakness for Dehra Dun then was a well known secret. He would visit this green town on any pretext as also on no pretext. He really loved spending a few relaxing days in the sylvan environs of its Circuit House where he would stroll across its expansive, wooded grounds or sit silently for hours under his favourite camphor tree with birds for companions, listening to their chirping. He didn't believe in mixing business with holidays, and in fact, discouraged any official or political engagements.

How I Met Malaviya

In the mid-1950s, as the Dehra Dun stringer for three mainstream English dailies viz *The Statesman*, *The Indian Express*, and *The Tribune*, I would often meet KD Malaviya on his frequent visits to town. At that time, there were just a handful of us journalists here; I was the youngest and academically the most qualified of the lot. At the time, I edited *Vanguard*, a local newsweekly, and regularly covered Malaviya's visits. Like Nehru, Malaviya too had a fondness for Dehra Dun and would often visit the town with his wife, Durga, for a weekend of rest and relaxation as well as to see his friends. Thus I found umpteen opportunities to meet him and was as such able to develop a personal rapport with him. With the birth of ONGC in August 1956, the scope of my news coverage from Dehra Dun vastly expanded. I had also made direct contact with some of the senior officers who had arrived in Dehra Dun to set up a suitable infrastructure for the newly born ONGC.

With *The Indian Express* in Delhi

I did not think twice when *The Indian Express* asked me to join as a reporter on its staff in Delhi. Even though the reporting of news in the capital was altogether a different ball game, I soon learned its nitty-gritty and made some useful contacts. I also visited Malaviya at his residence in Delhi on a couple of occasions. Mr Malaviya had by then taken a liking to me and extended to me his innate courtesy and hospitality. However, I was not destined to stay in Delhi for long. It so happened that I was selected via the Union Public Service Commission as the editor in the Directorate of Public Relations and Tourism, Himachal Pradesh that was then a Union territory. There too, I did not stay for more than 18 months.

...and I Became ONGC's PRO

ONGC then didn't have a public relations officer and when Malaviya asked me if I would like to join ONGC, I happily said 'Yes' for the simple reason that I would be posted in Dehra Dun. My father then did not keep good health and needed looking after.

However, destiny had willed otherwise. When I eventually joined ONGC in early 1961, I was promptly posted to Baroda. I demurred but Malaviya told me that Baroda was the happening place where I would find ample opportunity to make use of my journalistic talents. He was right to a large extent. We were just about half a dozen officers there, trying to set up the nucleus of regional headquarters that would look after the expanding exploration and allied operations in Gujarat. Fortunately, Ekbal Chand was the chief administrator in charge of the entire Western region. He had known me well enough from Dehra Dun and treated me like family. He called me one morning and wanted me to take up a few extra assignments such as labour relations, hospitality of the Russian expats and general coordination. I promptly agreed since all these new subjects were a good learning experience.

A Hands-on Minister

, Malaviya knew many of the officers by name as he himself had handpicked most of them. He never did flaunt his rank; on the contrary, he showed utmost courtesy and politeness. Malaviya was a hands-on chairman and would phone anyone if he needed to know something urgent or important. Thus all of us stayed alert and on our toes for we never knew when Malaviya's call might come. Malaviya would phone me if he wished to release a press statement from Delhi about some newsworthy development in Gujarat. It was then my job to dictate the draft press release to his secretary Nayyar who would take it down in shorthand.

In May 1961, there was a big blowout in Ankleshwar and Malaviya wanted to release the news from Delhi. I had the temerity to question his suggestion saying that a release from Delhi would be too late for the Gujarati press and it would then carry irresponsible news stories. Eventually, a via media was found and it was decided to release the news simultaneously from Delhi and Baroda. I hastily dictated the content to Nayyar, and a time was fixed for simultaneous release of the official version.

Labour Pains of a Different Kind

Both the Ankleshwar and Cambay projects had recruited hundreds of employees on contingent basis without observing any of the rules stipulated in the various labour enactments. Whenever and wherever large employers come, trade unions

follow them. The Baroda-based Sanat Mehta of Hind Mazdoor Sabha was the first to form the ONGC Employees' Union. A second ONGC Employees' Union under the aegis of the Indian National Trade Union Congress (INTUC) too appeared on the scene under the guidance of Ahmedabad-based Khandubhai Desai who was then a top INTUC leader. Each of the unions claimed to be the most accurate representative of the ONGC employees and sought formal recognition as such.

I had by then done enough homework on labour laws. I asked both the unions to submit, in writing, a list of their respective membership. Sanat Mehta promptly gave us a list of their members together with the receipts of membership fee. The INTUC union demurred and did not give me a point-blank answer. I wrote to the chief administrator, explaining to him the entire situation, and accorded, with his approval, official recognition to Sanat Mehta's union.

That greatly upset the redoubtable Khandubhai Desai who complained to Malaviya about me, accusing me of bias and partiality. So gullible was Malaviya that without even seeking a report from Baroda, he issued instructions for my transfer to Sibsagar in Assam. The Baroda journalists were aghast at my sudden transfer and sent a letter to the chief administrator demanding its cancellation. Sanat Mehta's trade union too, condemned my transfer. Even though I felt sad and betrayed, I did not protest and decided to join in Assam. In the interim, I went to Dehra Dun. Though my father had passed away, I still had a home there.

A Man of Honesty and Integrity

Despite this petty issue, I held Malaviya in high esteem; I loved him as I did my father. He was honest and sincere to a fault and no one could ever doubt his integrity. It was only due to his stubbornness and single-minded determination and devotion that India today boasts of a large number of national oil companies in upstream, downstream and even midstream sectors. He was truly the founder of the national oil industry in this country. Malaviya died on 27 May 1981. What an uncanny coincidence that his mentor, Nehru, had died on the same date in 1964.

CHAPTER 2

Patiala House in 1956

The number of ONGCians on 1 May 2006, was a massive 33,000, employed in its numerous work centres spread across the country.

However, like most organizations, ONGC too had made a small beginning. On 1 April 1956, there were barely 60 employees in the stately Patiala House. Within a year, by 1 April 1957, there was more than a sevenfold increase; the total strength then stood at 440.

Employees recruited in Calcutta waiting at Howrah Station to catch
their train for Dehra Dun.

Many among those employees had come from Calcutta,
specifically recruited by the Geological Survey of India (GSI),
for the Oil and Gas Division/Directorate. B Guha Roy, Amar
Nath Sen, Jyoti Bhushan Choudhary, Prabhat Ranjan Aich
and JJ Bhattasali were appointed on 14 December 1955.
Soon thereafter, Amar Nath Sen and Bhattasali were sent
to Dehra Dun. Sen was in the general administration and,
among other things, he assisted in the purchase of Patiala
House. Bhattasali, a selection grade stenographer, became
private secretary to AMN Ghosh.

Further recruitment was made and eight more newcomers
arrived in Dehra Dun on 16 August 1956—two days after
the birth of ONGC. Among them was ONGC's first woman
employee Abha Ball, a head assistant.

Besides the three of the seven earlier appointees, (Guha
Roy, Choudhary and Aich), others in that batch were the
Ganguli brothers, Preo Kumar and Amiya Kumar, Prithwish
Kumar Biswas and Santosh Kumar Saha. Earlier, three more
Calcutta recruits, PK Ganguly (a photographer) and two senior

assistants, HN Mazumdar and NK Natta had arrived in Dehra Dun to take up their respective assignments.

This then was the scenario at Patiala House in the first year of ONGC's birth. Bengali became the second most spoken language after Hindi.

Dehra Dun's Connaught Place

Soon enough, the Bengali *bhadralok* found their bearings in Dehra Dun that already boasted a fair sprinkling of their community. Much before the nationalization of life and general insurance, Bharat Insurance Company had built a three-storey residential complex on the left side of Chakrata Road as one walks down from the Clock Tower; it contained over 100 three-room flats. It was named Connaught Place; the insurance company fancied that its complex would some day rival New Delhi's famed namesake. The Life Insurance Corporation (LIC) inherited this large complex after the insurance business in India was nationalized. Across the road, Shanta Shumsher and Shashi Shumsher, the fabulously rich Rana brothers from Nepal, had earlier built an equally majestic complex, identical in design and façade, with two cinema houses as additional attractions.

The Kolkattans took up lodgings in some of the flats; there were more 'vacancies' than 'occupations' in those two residential buildings. The monthly rent of ₹40 seemed high at the time. A group of three married employees rented an independent flat while the bachelors shared the digs. The photographer, Ganguly, had rented a third-floor flat in the Nepalese Ranas' complex.

The Ranas had also built shops on the ground floor which, in due course, grew into a popular shopping centre. There were two photographers; Mela Ram and Narottam Chawla's Cinema Art Studios; Bata opened a retail outlet and Kesar Das Pahwa launched the town's first modern dry cleaning shop named Mercury. The *Vanguard*, then a weekly, set up its printing press there; I was its partner and editor.

Bengali Sweet Shop

What is of greater relevance, in the context of ONGC's history, is an eatery called Bengali Sweet Shop, on the ground floor of what was then called Connaught Hotel, built by well known transporter, Makhan Singh. The eatery's owner was Lalita Prasad Badoni, a handsome young man from Mussoorie.

Ganguly's flat was in close proximity to the Bengali Sweet Shop. Most of the bachelors would take their breakfast and dinner at Badoni's eatery; it was convenient, and the meals were wholesome and inexpensive. Badoni introduced fish dishes to cater to his increasing Bengali clientele; there were mutton preparations too. On most nights there would be 30 plus diners. Bengali customers would come for meals from as far as Hathibarkala and Raipur. Badoni's Bengali sweets were also in much demand. Mr AMN Ghosh was a regular customer. On Sundays, Ganguly and a couple of others would go down to Saharanpur and buy a basketful of fish for a mere 10 rupees. That was to be their special feast and picnic.

Abha Ball lived in a ground floor flat at the extreme end towards Bindal Bridge of the Bharat Insurance building. Her house became a 'communal kitchen'; the bachelors would troop in for their special meals, and they all shared the expenses. Bhattasali was one such bachelor who Abha was to marry later. The two served ONGC with distinction, and retired as joint directors several years ago.

Ganguly's flat, meanwhile, had become a transit accommodation of sorts; at one time or another, PK Chandra,

SC Roy Choudhury, KC Roy Choudhury, SK Das, KM Chandra—all geologists of the 1956 batch—stayed there until they found their regular lodgings. PK Chandra later rented a house on Nashvilla Road and lived there with his mother and sister. Fortunately, during those days, it was

SC Roy Choudhury   not difficult to find accommodation; and ONGCians were the preferred tenants. When Ganguly found that the water pipes in his flat leaked, the building's manager told him to shift to another flat; if the second flat too had some defective wiring, Ganguly was given the keys to a third flat. There were flats aplenty waiting to be rented out.

The Oil and Natural Gas Division had been set up as an appendage to the GSI, with just a handful of employees. A few months later, it was upgraded to a directorate. AMN Ghosh, MBR Rao, AK Dey were then senior geoscientists in GSI; they then made use of their offices, as also freely availed of the services of their staff for work relating to the formation of ONGC. As the ONGC-centric activities grew and some administrative staff was specifically recruited, a separate accommodation was allocated for the directorate in GSI's Chowringhee Road premises. As more employees were added, the available accommodation became constricted; in any case, it was a temporary arrangement.

A decision had already been taken to make Dehra Dun the headquarters of ONGC which was then in an embryonic state.

ONGC Finds a Permanent Home

The scene soon shifted from Chowringhee Road in Calcutta to Patiala House in Dehra Dun. Malaviya pointsman MBR Rao had earlier been sent to Dehra Dun to identify suitable premises for housing the headquarters of Oil and Natural Gas directorate. A message was then sent to the Surveyor General of India, Brig RH Wilson to help Rao in his search. The two inspected several buildings, but finally, their choice zeroed in on Patiala House, the stately mansion at 6, Young Road. It was promptly hired at the monthly rent of ₹2,500.

Patiala House had been purchased by Rajmata Bakhtawar Kaur, wife of His Highness Maharaja Bhupender Singh. The Rajmata later gifted the palatial Patiala House to her daughter Maharani Yadunandan Kumari, nicknamed Honey by the family. Honey married Col Raja Surender Singh of Nalagarh state, and became Rani of Nalagarh. Captain Amarinder Singh, the present chief minister of Punjab, is the grandson of Maharaja Bhupender Singh.

Thus Maharani Yadunandan Kumari was the owner when she sold the Patiala House on 2 April 1957, to the President of India. Those acquainted with the Constitution of India would know that all acts by the Government of India are carried out in the name of and at the pleasure of the President of India. That is how the President of India happened to become its purchaser. However, the official who signed the sale deed on behalf of the President was one PD Chawla, Executive Engineer, Central Public Works Department. The sprawling property, earlier known as Firland House, comprised the main Patiala House and several cottages built over a vast land area of 28 acres (nearly 1,33,299 square yards). There were over 700 litchi and mango trees. The Patiala House litchis were then considered amongst the most delicious grown in the Doon Valley.

.....and a Gold Mine

The total sale consideration was ₹6,20,000. The cost per square yard of the land alone came to approximately four rupees and 10 *annas*. The current land rate in the vicinity of Tel Bhawan is about ₹40,000 per square yard. Though ONGC did not find any oilfield in Dehra Dun, it did, however, discover a gold mine in Patiala House, which, by current valuation, must be worth more than ₹500 crores. Patiala House was merely the beginning. Within the following 20 years, ONGC was to buy or acquire hundreds of acres of land over which they built residential complexes and several impressive buildings. Among those are Keshava Deva Malaviya Institute of Petroleum Exploration (KDMIPE), Geodata Processing and Interpretation Centre (GEOPIC), ONGC Academy (initially named Institute of Management Development), Institute of Drilling Technology (IDT), Anveshan Bhavan, ONGC Officers Club, a Community Centre, a state of the art hospital and a large stadium, besides schools. All these acquisitions made ONGC, after Central and State governments, the single largest owner of real estate in Dehra Dun.

Everyone Cycled to Patiala House

ONGC made a humble start. Most employees, even the top brass, were humble. Almost all of them cycled their way to the office; there was a cycle stand at the rear of the main building that now houses the Subir Raha Museum; there was no scooter stand, since there were no scooters at that time. Only a handful of officers owned cars, and that didn't need dedicated parking. AMN Ghosh drove a Morris Minor; Ekbal Chand, ONGC's first secretary, would park his Standard 10 at the Patiala House's porch. The only relatively junior officer who owned a car was SN Talukdar; he was the proud owner of a Vanguard, in which he had driven all the way from Calcutta to join his new job at ONGC. BS Negi and BG Deshpande too cycled their way to their offices, while LP Mathur occasionally used the staff car, a nine-seater Willey's Station Wagon. Almost everyone in Patiala House remembered its registration number—UPS-4245. A creamish Dodge Station Wagon was bought in 1956. It was to remain the official workhorse of ONGC for the next 14 years. Malaviya and Ghosh would often use the Dodge to motor from Dehra Dun to Jwalamukhi. It was routinely used by successive chairmen.

MBR Bought a Landmaster

MBR Rao bought the first car, a Landmaster, in 1957. Next, LP Mathur and Dr Hari Narain purchased Ambassadors from Bagai Motors, Scindia House, Delhi. Hari Narain then paid ₹9,000 for a brand new car. BS Negi also bought an Ambassador.

The first among the 1956 batch to buy a car in 1960 was GC Aggarwal; he purchased a second-hand *Land Rover* for ₹2,000 from the father of Krishan Kant—one of the first chemists to join ONGC. PK Shrivastava became the second car owner when he bought a Fiat in 1961. Incidentally, Gautam Kohli was the first to have bought a Lambretta Scooter in 1956. Yet, the cycle stand continued to remain much in demand. Most employees, even gazetted officers, rode bicycles, albeit hired ones.

Houses were Aplenty

Like the earliest ONGCians from Calcutta, the batch of 1956 too, did not face any problem in finding suitable accommodation. In the initial three or four years of their careers, most of them spent as many as eight months with their respective field parties in various parts of the country.

So it was just for four months in a year that they needed some sort of accommodation. Finding a room in Dehra Dun was just a matter of few hours. *'We would arrive in town in our jeep-trailer, do a quick round of some "To-let" spots, and lo pronto the room was there. All of our worldly possessions were in the trailer; a suitcase or steel trunk, a holdall, folding chair and table besides a folding bed with mosquito net'*, says a young *pioneer*.

If the available accommodation offered more than a room, two or three of the young geoscientists shared it. The Jayal flats on New Road, in close proximity of the MKP College, attracted mostly Telugu speaking young men. The rent was barely ₹40. The more sensible among them would rent the flat for 12 months, with four of them paying ₹10 each. It was some place that they could call a home at least for a year. Sewak Ashram Road, at the rear of DAV College, was also a popular neighbourhood with many, as also Dalanwala with its bungalows built on large plots of land. They would be content with an annexe, or cottage, or even a part of the main bungalow with an independent entrance. Dr Inderjit Singh and Krishan Kumar, physicists of 1956 batch, initially stayed at the Doon Guest House (the Meedo Shopping Complex stands there today). Later they took cottages at 8 Curzon Road, where some of their batchmates had gravitated later. Gautam Kohli, after his marriage with Indira Rawlley, lived at 9 Curzon Road.

Incidentally, I then lived at 10 Curzon Road; thus Dr Singh, Kumar and others became my immediate neighbours and friends. Within a few months, almost the entire 1956 batch came to know me. PK Shrivastava continued to stay with his uncle at 8 Laxmi Road even after his marriage. Ekbal Chand, the first secretary, took on rent a big bungalow at 11 Lytton Road owned by GL Aggarwal who eventually retired as the President of the Forest Research Institute. AMN Ghosh and Dr Hari Narain were neighbours in the Race Course area. No wonder then, that the choice of Dehra Dun as the headquarters of ONGC was amply vindicated, thanks to the easy availability of accommodation. More importantly, it provided the appropriate environment for research and development activities vital to the growth of the industry.

Raj Kanwar in 1956

CHAPTER 3

ONGC: A Nehru Legacy

The formation of ONGC was one of the most durable and profitable legacies that had enriched India in many ways.

Nehru's life was inextricably linked with the history and destiny of modern India. As the first Prime Minister of Independent India for 17 uninterrupted years, Nehru's indelible imprint is seen in almost every field—be it economic, educational or social.

The creation of the national oil company in 1956, christened as ONGC, was Nehru's lasting legacy to his countrymen.

Though KD Malaviya had rightfully earned the sobriquet *'Father of Indian Petroleum Industry'*, it was Nehru's guidance and helping hand at every critical juncture that pulled ONGC through its teething troubles. Even the very idea of creating a separate petroleum division in 1955 had provoked strident opposition from powerful bureaucrats and politicians, egged on by Western petroleum lobbies. The multinational oil cartels tried their best to ensure that India did not venture into oil exploration on its own.

Another stratagem employed by them was to acquire, by hook or crook, petroleum exploration licences of large blocks in promising sedimentary basins in the Assam and Jaisalmer provinces which were then valid for a period of 40 years. The underlying objective was to keep those basins under their control with just a semblance of exploration activity so as to deny their access to other oil companies and, in particular, a national oil company. In fact, STANVAC had almost succeeded in obtaining a prospecting licence for Jaisalmer in 1954 with the active support of the then Rajasthan chief minister. Nehru was able to get that scuttled at the persistent goading of Malaviya.

Nehru always stepped in whenever the Planning Commission, or the Finance Ministry or the Petroleum Ministry (then known as the Ministry of Natural Science and Scientific Research), nitpicked at ONGC's financial proposals; Nehru invariably walked in as the guardian angel to wave his magic wand. Thus Malaviya and ONGC gradually went ahead. Nehru's support at every step was overpowering and crucial.

Nehru Nurtures ONGC

Putting ONGC on its feet was not the end of the story. Nehru continued to nurture ONGC in its years of infancy by

interacting with its top brass on each and every occasion. Nehru visited Dehra Dun in those years of ONGC's infancy. Later, he visited Cambay and Ankleshwar when the two fields struck oil. Nehru couldn't visit Jwalamukhi where ONGC had spudded its first well on 20 April 1957.

He nevertheless, made sure to send a special message, describing the event as a new and major step in search of oil, and the beginning of a great venture. Even in those early years, Nehru had realized the importance of oil, and declared that it was vital not only in the world economy but also in world politics.

The Cambay Discovery

The Cambay discovery had greatly enthused Malaviya and his team and propelled them to greater efforts. Nehru visited Cambay on 4 April 1960. He named the lucky rig Vijaya; as Nehru watched the crude oil flow, a few of its drops splotched his white *achkan*. Nehru was delighted, and declared that those drops symbolized the aspirations of the people of India. Nehru also visited ONGC offices and laboratories in Dehra Dun on quite a few occasions. Among those were Shanti Niketan at 103 Rajpur Road (that then housed the geophysical instruments laboratory) and the Naaz Building (where now Payal Cinema stands).

Nehru's visit in August 1957 to Dehra Dun provided a rare opportunity to the young geophysicists and geologists to interact

 with the great man. Everyone was asked to come in formal attire, a white Jodhpur coat with matching trousers. None possessed that formal dress; the Dehra Dun tailors worked overtime to stitch 200

suits; they were pleased with that unexpected bonanza and windfall. He addressed the young ONGCians and their senior mentors, and spoke about the great importance of their role in the venture of oil exploration.

Nehru and his Magic Wand

Nehru was always there, waving his magic wand whenever Malaviya and ONGC faced problems.

Everyone in the political and bureaucratic dispensation was aware of Nehru's unqualified support for him; that alone was enough to ensure ONGC a smooth passage. If Malaviya was the undisputed Father of Indian Oil Industry, Nehru was undoubtedly its godfather. Thousands, of ONGCians—those who are still active and others who retired after earning their spurs—would deferentially remember Nehru forever.

CHAPTER 4

The Teething Troubles

There was a beginning and that beginning today appears somewhat hazy.

What kind of labour pains did precede its birth? What was ONGC like in its infancy? How did it grow up through its teething troubles? Some of that needs to be retold today.

The embryonic precursor of ONGC was a separate petroleum division set up in 1955 in the GSI, Calcutta. Within a few months, this division got upgraded to Oil and Natural Gas directorate with an exclusive mandate; however, it continued to remain under the tutelage of GSI. The question is if GSI was ONGC's biological mother, who then was its biological father? By general consensus, KD Malaviya, the then minister of state for Mines and Oil in the government of Jawaharlal Nehru, was its biological father. Malaviya was a visionary, and like most visionaries, he also possessed a streak of obstinacy. In fact, he had already formulated a blueprint for setting up a national oil company in the public sector.

However, he went about this task gradually step by step thanks to the opposition he then faced from western oil companies who had had a vested interest in ensuring that India did not become even a minor oil producer; the Indian *babus* with a peculiar mindset of their own too put up the usual bureaucratic hurdles.

In Nehru's era, the Planning Commission was the sole repository of all wisdom in clearing and approving big projects. Thus the creation of a large public sector undertaking involving huge investments and uncertain returns presented an ideal opportunity to bureaucrats for fine-tuning their practice of nitpicking that over the years has been turned into a fine art.

Most western oil experts at that time had pooh-poohed at the likelihood of finding oil in India. A French expert, Monsieur Moulin was so confident about his prognostic that he openly wagered he would eat his boots if any oil was found in India. And when oil was eventually discovered in Ankleshwar in 1960, Malaviya asked his staff officers to find the whereabouts of the French expert and force him to eat an old pair of boots.

Comrade Kalinin

Against the vociferous opinion of western pessimists, Malaviya found succor in the report of noted Russian geologist

Mr NA Kalinin, recommending intensive and extensive exploration activity in all the, what are geologically termed, 'sedimentary basins' in the country.

But the antagonists dubbed Kalinin an adventurist and described as hasty, the decision of the government to set up a separate oil company. The protagonists of an independent national oil company, however, won the battle after Kalinin met Nehru and convinced him of the soundness of his recommendations. Thus the way was paved for the smooth delivery of ONGC.

...and ONGC is Born

The next logical step was the formal constitution of ONGC on 14 August 1956, under the suzerainty of Ministry of Oil and Mines, and the overall lordship of Malaviya, who also became its first chairman. Things were so different in those days that a minister could become the chairman of an undertaking

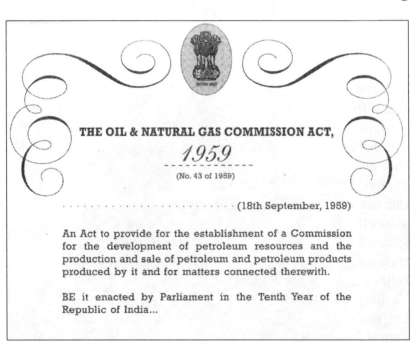

THE OIL & NATURAL GAS COMMISSION ACT,

1959

(No. 43 of 1959)

· (18th September, 1959)

An Act to provide for the establishment of a Commission for the development of petroleum resources and the production and sale of petroleum and petroleum products produced by it and for matters connected therewith.

BE it enacted by Parliament in the Tenth Year of the Republic of India...

under his ministry. Today a lowly joint secretary is put at the helm of an undertaking under a ministry if an exigent situation arises.

ONGC as a statutory undertaking was constituted on 15 October 1959 so as to give it a greater freedom in operations. But the politicians in power and their bureaucrat underlings continued to exercise enormous powers over ONGC by virtue of their file-pushing prerogatives. It was just as well that the chairmen of ONGC in the initial few years were men of eminence, mainly from the steel frame of Indian Civil Service (ICS), and as such managed to have their way. The ministerial minions thus could not flex their bureaucratic muscles.

Why Dehra Dun?

The present generation and the earlier one too must have often wondered about the why behind the selection of Dehra Dun as the headquarters of a national organization such as ONGC. I too have been repeatedly asked this question even during my visits abroad. There was very little likelihood of oil being discovered in and around Dehra Dun though a lone well was test drilled at Mohand, albeit without any success. The most known oil reserves were then only in Assam. It is a different matter that later Gujarat also turned out to be a major source. But why Dehra Dun? Nehru even in mid–1950s had realized that Delhi was getting overcrowded and that new offices and organizations must not be set up in the capital, (it is a pity that the succeeding political dispensations did not respect Nehru's considered opinion.) Once Nehru's views became known, some influential UP Congress leaders lobbied for Rampur as the headquarters of ONGC. As bait, they had also offered the use of one of the palaces and some other buildings owned by the *Nawab* of Rampur.

Barrister JM Chatterji was then one of the most respected citizens in Dehra Dun. He lived in a sprawling bungalow on Lytton (now Subhash) Road. In 1942, during the Quit India movement, KD Malaviya, as an underground rebel, had taken shelter in Chatterji's house and ever since, the two remained friends till the end. Mahavir Tyagi was then a deputy defence minister. The two were Malaviya's mutual friends. They strongly lobbied for Dehra Dun.

The plus points were obvious: proximity to Delhi, an excellent school network and a salubrious climate. Malaviya needed no convincing; Nehru's fondness for Dehra Dun too was well-known (remember that he was imprisoned in Dehra Dun jail during the Independence movement) and he too readily endorsed Dehra Dun. The issue then was signed, sealed and delivered. Thus thanks to two veteran Doonites, Dehra Dun was put on the world oil map.

CHAPTER 5

A Nucleus of Oilmen

*D*ehra Dun of 1956 was a quiet place with pleasant *climate and plenty of greenery. Away from the noise and rat race of a big city, it was pensioners' paradise.*

Cultural and educational facilities of a very high order catered to the needs of its cosmopolitan inhabitants drawn from all parts of India. There was also a touch of aristocracy with scores of mini palaces on large plots of land. One such palace was the famous Patiala House that was later to become the headquarters of ONGC. Institutions of repute, such as The Indian Military Academy, modelled after the Royal Military Academy of Sandhurst, England and the Forest Research Institute were Dehra Dun's top attractions.

In the pre-independence days, Dehra Dun was the home of and a safe haven for freedom fighters. Malaviya came in the latter category. Post-independence, the cool heights of Mussoorie was the favourite destination of Nehru and his family, and of the elite seeking to escape the heat and dust of Delhi. En route lay the charming link of Dehra Dun whose landscape combined the advantages of both a hilly country and the plains. More importantly, Delhi was getting suffocated with a multitude of government offices and organizations, and any more such additions there would only impose further strain on the socio-economic fabric which was already fraying at the edges. Dehra Dun, just 240 kilometers and six hours away by road from Delhi was an attractive alternative. This was then the alternative that was finally agreed on for the setting up of ONGC Headquarters.

Enter Rookie Drillers

Malaviya had the entire blueprint mapped in his mind. By middle of May 1955, he had the nucleus of the ONGC directorate in place. The advertisements, calling for the largest ever recruitment of geologists and geophysicists, were published in newspapers, and the selection process by the Union Public Service Commission had begun. One headache, however, remained. In one of his diaries, Malaviya would lament in exasperation: '...*How do I convince the UPSC that there are no oil well drillers in the country? They think that an ordinary plumber or a tubewell drilling contractor can be an oil well driller.*' A tubewell rig might look like a miniature oil drilling rig but that's where the resemblance ended. Take into account the enormity of an oil rig; the great depths to which it drilled, deeper and deeper in the unknown and unseen bowels of the earth, and the dangers of encountering high pressure and high temperature zones. All of that demanded extraordinary skills and knowledge that a semi-skilled tubewell driller would not and could not possibly possess.

Drilling was as crucial to the oil industry as a steering wheel is to an automobile. Malaviya realized that if there were no drillers, there would be no drilling. And if there was no drilling, there would be no oil. 'After all, oil is where you find it', says the industry wisdom.

There were no formal training schools or colleges for drillers. They came from varied backgrounds; many of them were loud, brash and easily prone to anger because of the back-breaking work carried out in some of the most inhospitable terrains. Legend has it, that roughnecks earned the name from the rough and calloused necks and shoulders that were a result of pushing and lifting heavy loads. The roustabouts, as the name suggests, were required to do just about everything.

The oil industry at that time was not so developed in the country that one could go about recruiting drillers with ease. Malaviya knew about the difficulty. In his letter to Maulana Azad on 20 August 1954, he spelt out his ideas. *'Drilling technique is already known to us. You, perhaps, know that the best drillers that Assam Oil Company possessed are Indians, and I will not hesitate to contact them for getting their help and gaining knowledge and experience when time comes.'* He was also aware of the fact that a large majority of foreign workers in the British controlled Anglo-Iranian Oil Company in Iran, during the 1930s were Indians. He had planned to poach them. To lure the experienced drillers from the oil companies, he had suggested higher pay scales in his original proposal. The government had shot that down, denying Malaviya that extra bit of a carrot.

They learnt on the job; hard labour brought out the rough in them, and over the years, myths and legends had built around the rustic lifestyle of drillers. In over a hundred years, they had turned into a cult. Millions of dollars worth rigs operated on their judgement and commitment to do the job right. A single mistake cost very dearly to the companies. Malaviya was well aware of this aspect of drilling. He wanted an educated lot to take out the rough edge.

Malaviya—The Dreamer

Malaviya was not only a big dreamer but also possessed the determination to fulfill those dreams. He could foresee the growing number of oil rigs and the necessity of building up a sizable cadre of drillers. But where was he to find such educated drillers?

After some persuasion, Malaviya was able to obtain a no-objection certificate from UPSC permitting the ONGC directorate to recruit drillers directly. He asked the GSI stalwarts to let the word out—that they were looking for oil well drillers with a good educational background and some practical experience. The wanabe drillers responded. By the beginning of February 1956, they started trickling in. KC Chandra, with a B.Sc. degree and some practical experience with Indian Bureau of Mines, walked in to face the venerable AMN Ghosh. The first question Ghosh asked was, 'Can you do hard, physical labour?' Chandra nodded. He was taken in. MD Nautiyal, VK Arora, SK Das, IB Roy, Digin Ray, RS Morton and Inderjit Singh Bhai followed. Nautiyal was from IIT Kharagpur and Arora from Delhi College of Engineering. They all joined as drilling assistants and were promptly sent off to Assam Oil Company for on-the-job training.

AOC grew on hoary traditions, which it naturally treasured with much pride. In 1950s, the number of Indian drillers manning its rigs had substantially risen. Most of the British drillers had returned home, leaving much of the drilling operations in the hands of Indians. Even earlier, in any case, Indians were predominant among the middle and lower rungs of drilling crews; the Englishmen manned only top few positions, those of drilling superintendent or tool pushers.

Digboi and Nahorkatiya were the destinations. The Digboi oilfield had the distinction of being one of the oldest in the world. They were assigned different shifts—eight hours every day with no break. Night shifts always seemed the longest. They all had to start from scratch. In those times, as now, hiring a driller was not like one-stop shopping. It was an arduous process starting with roughnecks. They handled huge tubulars as well as other heavy equipment that travelled at breakneck speed and suddenly stopped in seconds. When they came back to the camp, they were a tired lot with blackened faces and greasy work overalls. The next baptism was of derrickmen. Standing on a narrow platform at a height of 90 feet, they had to free the long tubulars from the jaws of the holding tongs, and drag them to the storage position. It was a scary sight with the derrickman standing two feet away from the 200-tonne string travelling at blinding speed. Their lives depended on the alertness of the driller controlling the brake mechanism.

The rookie drillers found only a handful of expat drillers. Among the older Indian drillers were QT Rehman, Lahiri, Deka, Bhuyan and some others. There were also a few younger drillers and they included AK Mitra, AK Chandra, A Chandwani and Hiro Khushalani. Rehman joined ONGC as a superintending drilling engineer. Bhuyan and Deka too joined ONGC in Assam as senior drillers. All the three retired within a few years.

AK Mitra too crossed over to ONGC as a senior driller (shot-hole). Subsequently, he was promoted, via the UPSC, as senior driller (deep drilling). Mitra's tenure in ONGC was the longest among the AOC drillers; he retired only in 1989 as the first director of the Institute of Drilling Technology. In his long and eventful career, Mitra had occupied some top positions, and was involved in many an important milestone such as Ankleshwar, Aliabet and later Bombay High.

LP Mathur, with his AOC background, visited them during the training. The first thing he invariably asked was: 'How many times do you go up to the Monkey Board?' (that narrow platform at a height of 90 feet.) He was satisfied only when he was told that it was a normal routine to go up three to four times during a shift. He was simply testing their mettle, as also their battle readiness.

When the drillers came back after six months, they had been promoted as assistant drillers. On reaching Calcutta, they were asked to undergo a crash course in the Russian language. An Indian lady taught them Russian, following which they were given ₹1,000 each to buy enough warm clothes. They were to go to Russia for training in drilling technology for two years. It was towards the middle of 1956. The directorate had graduated into a commission on 14 August. They heard about 150 odd apprentices undergoing crash courses in geology and geophysics in Calcutta, and also came across a few of those wide-eyed young geoscientists. A feeling of bonding blossomed among the furure colleagues, and they started believing themselves to be members of a larger family.

Malaviya and Ghosh met them in the Parliament House annexe on the eve of their departure. Malaviya underscored the importance of their mission, and asked them to be good ambassadors. He wished them good health and Godspeed. Ghosh asked them, in a fatherly manner, to learn well and take care so as not to fall ill.

Baku—Oil Capital of the Soviet Union

Tagiev, ONGC's Russian drilling consultant, met them in Moscow, and informed them of the training schedule. After a while, they travelled southwards to the oil capital, Baku. If Baku had impressed Malaviya, it was to overwhelm the rookie drillers in every way. For some, Baku was the experience of a lifetime.

Baku in 1950s

Baku is the capital of Azerbaijan, a province of the erstwhile Soviet Union and one of the most important ports of the Caspian Sea (geologically speaking, it is actually a lake). Home to a cultured, friendly and hospitable people, Azerbaijan had the legacy of a rich oil history stretching back to 1,300 AD. In the early years of the twentieth century, it had the distinction of being the world's largest producer of oil. Baku was a town with a soul; its aristocratic houses, narrow lanes and numerous fruit vendors world reminded visitors of many historic cities in India.

Hotel Ostankino became their home. As official state guests, Indian drillers were extended all courtesy and hospitality. They got 40 rubles per month as pocket money. Professor Saftarkulif had a well designed curriculum for them. They were taken to Neftekamsk for practical training. The professor became so proficient in English that at the end of the year, he ended up compiling a Russian-English translation booklet. That would help all future ONGCians. As it turned out, their stay was not about work alone.

The news about the arrival of this young lot of drillers from India slowly spread across Baku. It was for the first time that Baku residents met Indians; they liked what they saw and took a fancy to the unostentatious visitors. Vivekananda, Gandhi and Nehru were already revered names; Raj Kapoor with movies like *Shri 420* and *Awaara,* revolving around the life of a rustic hero, with a heart of gold, had touched the hearts of the Russians and other nationalities, across the Soviet Union. Baku was no exception. The young Indians thus became the toast of Baku. They started receiving invitations for social and cultural functions at universities and schools.

Drillers took Malaviya's farewell advice of becoming good ambassadors rather seriously; love was in the air.

At those functions, they met the girls (*devushkas*) and turned them into girlfriends (*podrugas*). Digin Ray was the first to be smitten; four others caught the infection. Before love could come to fruition, they were abruptly called back to India at the end of one year. They were asked to return on 28 November 1957. The marriages got registered just one or two days before their departure for India. Their wives stayed behind. It was cruel to the newly married. However, India needed them more.

A storm awaited the bridegrooms in the person of AMN Ghosh. When Ghosh flew into a rage, it was prudent to leave the nearby corridors. And, he was plain mad, absolutely mad. The non-marriage clause was not in the drillers' undertaking; but breaching the unwritten covenant was unacceptable. He threatened to make all drill sites non-family postings. They were immediately sent off to Hoshiarpur. Inderjit Singh Bhai was sacked as he had not only lied about his marital status in his passport, but had also faked his dubious qualifications. The commission brooked no indiscipline. The non-marriage clause was introduced as an addendum in all the subsequent 'undertakings' to be given by employees going abroad for training.

The Russian Wives

This first batch of drillers would spread out to all corners of the country to successfully take over the operations from the foreigners. In a year or two, their Russian wives arrived in India. Janette joined Digin in Hoshiarpur and Tatyana reunited with Chandra in Sibsagar. The brides of the other three were left behind in Baku; perhaps they had had second thoughts, or more likely, had not been permitted by the local authorities to leave the USSR. Those were really extraordinary times.

A drilling rig with all its ancillaries occupied an area of approximately 250 square meters. But, the driller needed the help of the geo scientists to pinpoint the general location to him. The young pioneers were almost ready to scour the length and breadth of the country to get the best possible locations for the drillers.

Pinpointing an exact location was, and still remains, like picking a needle in a haystack.

120 Young Pioneers

Not too many readers of the mainstream English newspapers would have noticed a single column advertisement published by the UPSC on 19 May 1956. It was the kind of advertisement that UPSC routinely issued by the dozen, inviting applications for gazetted jobs in the Central Government.

A total of 52 apprentice geologists and 77 apprentice geophysicists were sought to be recruited. Those were not the run-of-the mill jobs that would attract applicants in droves. The minimum prescribed academic qualifications were a second-class master's or an equivalent honours degree in geology. Even a diploma in geology and applied geology from the Indian School of Mines and Applied Geology was considered acceptable. Inadvertently, the advertisement had overlooked prescribing the required academic qualifications for the post of apprentice geophysicist. The oversight was realized soon enough. A few days later, the UPSC came out with a corrigendum prescribing the academic qualifications for geophysicists. A second-class master's or equivalent honours degree in exploration geophysics or physics or radio physics and electronics or applied mathematics were stipulated.

At that time, about 12 universities offered courses for master's degree in geology. Those were Aligarh, Madras, Andhra, Osmania, Nagpur, Lucknow, Benaras, Presidency College in Calcutta, Mysore, Bombay, Baroda and Saugar. But hardly any university offered geophysics as a subject though Banaras University taught it as part of geology while Andhra University's meteorology course covered oceanography and physics as part of the earth's interior. It was an unpopular subject with little or no job prospects.

There was another unusual feature. The UPSC did not disclose the name of the employer, leaving the 'hopefuls' for these jobs in suspense. There was no ONGC at that time; only its nucleus had been set up in the form of an oil and gas directorate as an appendage to GSI. In order to ensure that the advertisement evoked good response, the employer advised the UPSC to request some select universities to recommend eligible candidates from amongst their students or alumni. Incidentally, it was perhaps for the first time that the UPSC had taken such an unusual step of directly soliciting applications from universities and thus it became the precursor to what are today called campus interviews or recruitment.

UPSC Becomes the Recruiter

Even if the would-be-employer had been named in the UPSC advertisement, many of the qualified applicants would not have felt enthused. The advertisement, at best, had cause curiosity. Most of the eligible candidates were attracted only because of the label of class one gazetted posts, irrespective of the identity of the employer. At that time, and to some extent even today, the holders of class one gazetted jobs occupied a higher pedestal both in society in general, and in the matrimonial market in particular.

Therefore, the advertisement evoked much more than the expected response. The universities too had made a large number of recommendations. And there must have been more than six to seven hundred direct applications including a large number from those serving in the various government departments, albeit at relatively junior levels.

Though a formal decision to set up ONGC had been taken by the government, its birth came a few months later. However, KD Malaviya, in his *avatar* as minister of state for mines and oil, and the likely chairman of yet to be born ONGC, directed MBR Rao to immediately start recruitment of over 120 young men with master's degrees in geology and geophysics. Rao was then the chief geophysicist in the GSI; he took prompt action to comply with Malaviya's directions and formally wrote to the UPSC for the recruitment of the required number of young men with the stipulated educational qualifications.

Looking back at the sequence of events in 1956, it is clear that the recruitment for these posts was given top priority. Setting aside the proverbial red tape, the UPSC greatly accelerated an otherwise lengthy process and completed the given task in record time.

Just consider the following:

- UPSC advertised the jobs on 19 May with 9 June 1956 as the last date for the receipt of applications. The time schedule for submission of applications was just about three weeks.

- The corrigendum prescribing the educational qualifications for the post of geophysicist was issued a week later, with the last date for the receipt of applications remaining unchanged, viz., 9 June 1956.

- A week after the deadline for the receipt of applications ended, the UPSC started inviting the shortlisted candidates for interviews giving them just enough time to reach the UPSC office at Dholpur House, Shahjahan Road, New Delhi.

- The interviews were spread over a period of nearly six weeks. Two batches, each comprising 10 candidates, were interviewed daily, in morning and afternoon sessions.

- The interviews were completed by end of July 1956.

- Offers of appointment were signed by AMN Ghosh, then Director of Oil and Natural Gas Directorate. The successful candidates were directed to report to Ghosh at the office of GSI, 27 Chowringhee Road, Calcutta, between 16 and 20 August 1956.

- Thus the entire process, beginning with publication

of the advertisement by the UPSC on 19 May 1956 and ending with the date of reporting on duty took less than three months. These fast-track interviews, selections, offers of appointment and date of joining within a period of three months would be considered a miracle of sorts by the mandarins of today.

In the backdrop of the fact that ONGC was born on 14 August 1956, it was not a mere coincidence that most of the 120 odd young men, with first class master's degrees in geology, physics or geophysics and mathematics were in their training classes in Calcutta within a week of ONGC's birth. That was the end result of a systematic strategy, conceived and initiated by Malaviya himself. Thus began the exciting odyssey of those young pioneers.

CHAPTER 6

When the Russians Landed

*N*O *account of the early days of ONGC will be complete without dwelling upon the international flavour provided by Russian experts and drillers.*

They came in droves as ONGC then did not have its own trained manpower. To begin with, nearly 100 Russians arrived. Many of them lived and worked in Dehra Dun. Others moved over to projects such as Cambay, Ankleshwar, and later, Sibsagar. At each project there were separate bungalows or guest houses for the Russian experts, and also special Russian messes.

It was the Stalin era in the erstwhile Soviet Union; the Russians, though vocal did not talk politics. It was believed that a few KGB operators too had been smuggled with the Russian contingent, ever ready to inform on their compatriots if any indiscretion was committed.

N Chaman was then one of the most well-known figures in Dehra Dun. He had begun his business with a dairy and later graduated to become a restaurateur and hotelier. At the time, owned Indiana Restaurant in Astley Hall. Chaman also had had the distinction of starting White House, Dehra Dun's first decent hotel. Ekbal Chand of the IAS, from its Hyderabad cadre, became ONGC's first and perhaps only secretary. Soon, he became friendly with Chaman. Their common interest was rum and rummy.

A Guest House for Russians

Chaman was persuaded by Ekbal Chand to accommodate the Russian experts and to look after their boarding and lodging needs. Thus the first international guest house in Dehra Dun with a mess came into existence. The Russians were initially accommodated at 7 Inder Road, a large property which Chaman had then purchased. (He himself then lived at 49, East Canal Road, near Dwarka Stores). A few of the Russians had brought their wives; some of them did their own cooking but others partook their meals either in the mess or would take an evening walk to Indiana in Astley Hall to have a vodka sundowner that occasionally continued late into the night. Though the Russians received their vodka courtesy the Soviet embassy, their quota was not enough.

Indian Vodka

When their stock was spent, they all implored Chaman to do something about its replenishment. For once, the otherwise resourceful Chaman was at his wits' end. Being a regular visitor to Indiana and having close relations with the Chaman family, I sometimes joined this group. One of the Russians was once polite enough to offer me vodka which I drank on the rocks as was customary. So I knew how the vodka tasted. Chaman (whom I respectfully addressed as *Mamaji*) sought my help. I suggested white Indian country liquor that tasted much like vodka, or so I thought.

Chaman took the hint and told the Russians that he could get some Indian vodka for them. The Russians were surprised but nevertheless happy at the prospect of having some vodka, even an Indian one. 'Do you have Indian Vodka?', they asked in unison. '*Da, da*', Mamaji replied with glee in Russian of which he had picked up a few words. '*Kharasho, ochen kharasho*', they joyously shouted.

Soon a waiter was dispatched to the *Machhi* Bazar country liquor *theka* (shop) and he returned with 12 bottles of the Indian vodka. At that time, the standard of country liquor was much better and most of them, in fact took a liking to that drink, laced with fresh lime. Thus began the Russians' long courtship with our *desi* vodka and thereafter there was never, ever any shortage of vodka for our guests.

Ekbal Chand

And finally, a few words about Ekbal Chand. He originally belonged to Nizam Civil Service but after the merger of Hyderabad with the Indian Union, he, together with other civil servants, was absorbed in the IAS. Thus he came to be posted at ONGC and took up residence at 11 Lytton Road, then owned by the late KL Aggarwal, President of Forest Research Institute (and father of Dr Anil Aggarwal).

His demeanour was aristocratic. He was an excellent administrator and set about the task of giving ONGC a sound administration. His office table was always neat and clean, never any pending file. He would come to office on time and depart exactly at 5 p.m. A friendly and helpful man, and soon became a popular member of Dehra Dun society. He was fond of the good things of life and was always a generous host. Soon, I became a welcome and frequent visitor to his house that he liked to call his castle.

CHAPTER 7

Bombay High

*P*roduction from Bombay High commenced on *21 May 1976 with much fanfare. For the past 42 years or so, it has been in a declining trajectory which of course is a natural phenomenon in most mature oil and gas fields worldwide.*

ONGC has nevertheless been making a sustained effort to reverse its decline, and have succeeded to some extent, thanks to the innovative techniques and technology introduced under the stewardship of the then Director Offshore TK Sengupta. As a consequence, Western Offshore fields enhanced their production volume by 14.6 per cent during financial year of 2015, as compared to the previous financial year.

At its peak, Bombay High had produced 150 MMbbl in 1998 that then constituted the bulk of India's domestic oil output. It is still ONGC's best milch cow, nay, golden goose. Today, it would be interesting to recall those heady days in May 1976 when a group of determined and innovative men headed by an obsessive workaholic chairman, NB Prasad, put the Bombay High field on commercial production. Prasad had been appointed chairman of ONGC on 10 April 1974 with a mandate to 'Put Bombay High on commercial production in the shortest possible time', and was literally given a blank cheque and the rank of a secretary to the Government of India.

Prasad took this mandate very seriously and set about planning how best and how fast he could start oil production from Bombay High. The Indians in general, and ONGC in particular, had put much hope on the success of this prolific oilfield discovered on the western coast. Prasad was a hands-on chairman, if there was one, and led from the front. Everyone involved in the operations worked round-the-clock. Off and on days were not sacrosanct, and even the shift hours were flexible. They were all there in their flaming orange overalls with Prasad in command. HS Cheema, whom Prasad had brought in from Engineers India Ltd. (EIL), was the general manager (operations), an adjutant general of sorts. SP Rao Janamanchi who came later from EIL, was put in charge of construction. Others involved in operation Quick Production were ONGC veterans of 1956-59 vintage; LL Bhandari, SK Manglik, Hugh Aranha, SS Paintal as well as a few others. There were also scores of subalterns and foot soldiers with varied roles and responsibilities.

Strangers to Offshore Technology

Consider the situation that existed 42 years ago. Almost everyone, with a couple of honourable exceptions, was a stranger to offshore technology in general and production techniques in particular—they were as different from onshore production as chalk is from cheese. Yet, Prasad and his team of daredevils, by sheer grit, indomitable spirit and youthful exuberance, successfully overcame their relative inexperience.

Thus, by starting commercial production from Bombay High, those daredevils buried deep the myth about India's inability in undertaking offshore exploration, so invidiously built and propagated by western oil cartels.

Preparations were afoot for weeks before for this momentous event. A Single Buoy Mooring system (SBM) was installed near Production Platform 'A'; a tanker, with a storage capacity of over 85,000 tonnes and speed of 15 knots, was moored to the SBM. The tanker was aptly named MV Jawaharlal Nehru, who had not lived to see the fulfillment of his dream. The platform was, in turn, connected to SBM through sub-sea pipelines. Oil was to flow into the pipeline after separation of water. The associated gas was to be flared. The SBM system was connected to the tanker Jawaharlal Nehru.

Baldev Singh, who retired as general manager (production), was then in charge of the tanker and responsible for ensuring its smooth operations. On 3 May 1976, Singh's team, comprising Ravindran and HP Vanjara, found the wheel of the master gate valve that was installed on the well jammed. It was a day before the trial run of oil to the tanker via the SBM. Singh added his own physical force to that of Ravindran and Vanjara but without success.

In Flight
Bombay - Delhi

प्रधान मंत्री भवन
PRIME MINISTER'S HOUSE
NEW DELHI

February 13, 1984

Dear Shri Baldev Singh,

Our time on the BHS was all too brief. I am sorry I was not able to go around the rig, to see it for myself and to meet and talk with the personnel who are living there.

As you know my programme had to be curtailed because of the Moscow visit - I leave soon after arrival in Delhi and for just under 24 hours!

You and your men are doing important work, far from home and in difficult circumstances. I am sure you are all aware of how vital it is to our economy and to our security.

Please convey my good wishes to them all.

Yours sincerely,

(Indira Gandhi)

Shri Baldev Singh,
Field Production Superintendent,
Bombay Offshore Project,
ONGC, Express Tower,
Nariman Point,
Bombay

Fortuitously, SK Manglik, Project Manager, arrived (Manglik retired as the first C&MD of ONGC on 30 April 1995). He casually asked, 'Anything you need?' Without hesitation, Singh requested Manglik to lend his helping hand in moving the jammed wheel. The combined torque strength of the group succeeded in moving it.

'Thus we obtained the first drop of Bombay High oil on 4 May', Singh told his friends later. Rao Janmanchi has another interesting anecdote. 'The deadline for the production of crude was fast approaching. One evening, Chairman Prasad called me to his hotel suite, and over scotch, underlined the criticality of the operation'. Janmanchi moved to the barge where Prasad too later set up his base. A chopper brought office files to the barge. Thus, for all practical purposes, the barge had become a virtual Operations Room.

An Ambitious Target

Prasad and his core team had set themselves a short time frame of two years for commencing production from Bombay High. It was an ambitious target, not achieved under similar conditions anywhere else in the world. What made matters worse was that hardly a few in the core team knew about oceanography, barring Cheema. Chairman Prasad showed the knack of picking the right people for the right job. HP Arahna was the production man. SK Manglik, AP Anand, SS Paintal and several others were in his team. Likewise SM Malhotra, SC Mittal and KS Shanker formed the core team of the drillers. They were among the best in ONGC. But their selection on the core teams had a caveat: perform or else you will be shunted out.

Quickly starting production was easier said than done. That meant ONGC needed to drill more and more wells, which in turn meant that it must have additional rigs to drill. Drilling alone was not the end. One needed to set up a quick fix production system in order to produce oil from the newly drilled wells. But that too was not the end of the story. The next step was to bring the oil to surface, establish storage and transportation facilities. And finally, identify a refinery to refine the produced oil. There were several links in this chain. And each link was as important as the next one.

It was this daunting task that Prasad and his team faced. How they accomplished this remarkable feat in the astounding time of two years is another story that needs to be told some time.

Petroleum Minister KD Malaviya's visit to Shenandoah rig on 2 May 1976

It was 0243 hours on 21 May 1976. Platform 'A' was manoeuvered into a place in the lower half of the template, thereby completing the assembling process. Shenandoah awaited a little distance away. When the time approached, Shenandoah was brought closer to the Platform. It was clockwork precision; the floor of the rig slid over Well #A2 that was waiting to be produced. A Christmas tree was installed; everyone waited with bated breath.

At 0955 hours, the valve was opened. Through the pipeline, the oil flowed to the SBM, and then it was pumped to the tanker. All eyes were riveted on the pressure gauges, wondering if there were any leaks.

The master of the tanker signaled 'All Okay'. The Bombay High oil had finally reached the tanker for onward transportation to the refinery. Later, Well #A1 was also connected. The combined oil production from the two wells was 4,300 barrels that day. Subsequently, the output was raised to 7,500 barrels per day. And that marked the end of part one of Phase One Operation.

So stern was Prasad on the laid down time schedule, that a few hours delay in the commercial production cast its shadow on jubilation and celebrations. Nevertheless, that was a great achievement, and congratulations poured in from everywhere. Prime Minister Indira Gandhi sent a special message of congratulations. Minister Malaviya was most effusive in his message praising the herculean effort of ONGC. Even today, in its twilight years, Bombay High is the golden goose both for ONGC and India and it is still ONGC's best bet.

CHAPTER 8

Sagar Samrat: ONGC's Lucky Mascot

*F*orty four years after the first well in Bombay High
was spudded, it will be interesting to recall the story
of Sagar Samrat—ONGC's indefatigable workhorse.

Sagar samrat was the first offshore rig that ONGC had bought.
It arrived in the Indian waters in May 1973 and started drilling
in February 1974.

Since then it has drilled one well after another—a total of
130 wells in the course of its lifespan of 28 years—probably
a world record. To it also goes the credit of discovering 14
major structures and adding three billion metric tonnes of
reserves to India's oil kitty. Though formally retired, the old
workhorse, even today, provides living accommodation and
power backup facilities.

In the early 1950s, when India was still wrestling
with numerous post-Independence teething troubles, the
discovery of oil within the country had assumed utmost
urgency. As written elsewhere, there were many prophets
of doom, particularly among the western experts, who then
predicted that Indian sedimentary basins were devoid of any
hydrocarbon reservoirs.

ONGC was set up in August 1956 as a national oil
company amidst this widespread scepticism. However, to

its credit, ONGC belied all those gloomy predictions, and made its first discovery in Cambay, in September 1958. That was followed by discovery of oil in Ankleshwar on 14 May 1960. A hat-trick of discoveries was performed when oil was struck near Rudrasagar, Assam, in December 1960.

In the meantime, the consumption for petroleum products in the country continued to gallop at a rapid pace, touching about 15 million metric tonnes (MMT) in 1968 while the total domestic production was about six MMT. ONGC had drawn up an ambitious 10-year plan that envisaged reaching a production level of 10 MMT with 4.5 MMT coming from offshore. Thus offshore exploration became a desperate necessity. The Bombay High oilfield had already been identified as a potential reservoir, and it needed to be developed. However, identifying a suitable offshore drilling rig, and drilling expertise was a tough task that unfortunately neither ONGC nor its Soviet consultants then possessed.

What was the Way Out?

To make matters worse, there were many sceptics who spurned the very idea of going offshore; they declared that neither India possessed enough resources, nor the expertise to venture into offshore operations.

What was, then, the way out? The promising Bombay High oilfield lay under a water depth of 260 to 300 feet.

The Russians were out of depth in deep drilling technology. Their limited experience was in the shallow waters off the Caspian Sea. With their help, ONGC had earlier drilled its first offshore well at Aliabet. Only the western companies at that time possessed the technology of drilling in deeper waters. In 1950s, 20 meters were considered deep waters. A decade later, as the technology developed, 300 meters and beyond became the deep waters. Fast rising oil consumption at home forced the Americans to explore the tough Alaskan oil while Britain was about to start exploration in the North Sea. Newer offshore technologies were rapidly being introduced. Nearly 200 offshore rigs operated worldwide at the end of 1960s.

Worldwide Shortage of Offshore Rigs

There was a worldwide shortage of offshore rigs. The major multinationals as such were interested only in looking at big finds and didn't evince much interest in India. Instead, a few small western independents offered to conduct the exploration and exploitation of Bombay High. Their offers included several hidden costs. Malaviya, however, was much averse to handing over the prolific Bombay High field to foreign companies.

Happily, there was also an offer from the Japanese. Mitsubishi had roped in Offshore International S.A. (OISA) that was then credited with having designed the world's first jack-up in 1954. Together, the two companies offered to build a mobile drilling rig at competitive prices. It was thus left to the ONGC Chairman at the time, Leslie Johnson, to undertake a techno-economic evaluation of the Japanese proposal; a committee was accordingly formed to look into its pros and cons. As the committee dithered on its choice between jack-up and semi-submersible, Johnson lost his patience, took the matters into his own hands and decreed in favour of jack-up.

However, before a final decision could be taken, Johnson demitted office on 7 September 1970. His successor Balwant Singh Negi incidentally was the first ONGC insider to have been elevated to the coveted post of its chairman, albeit in acting capacity. A geophysicist from the stable of GSI, Negi was widely known for his pusillanimity and dithering. *'Negi was a stickler for rules and regulations and lacked the aggressive drive of leadership and qualities of effective man management so very essential in giving proper direction to a vibrant organization,'* wrote Iqbal Farooqi in his book *The Story of ONGC*. However, it was altogether a different Negi who then showed uncharacteristic resoluteness and courage in handling the delicate and complex negotiations with the Japanese.

ONGC Orders a *Samrat*

In February 1971, ONGC, or rather the Indian government, placed an order on Mitsubishi for a self-propelled jack-up drilling rig, costing the then princely amount of 1,270 crores (12.70 billion). Though the delivery period was two years, Negi did not allow grass to grow under his feet and stationed two top-ranking engineers, HGT Woodward and AK Mitra, in the historic city of Hiroshima in Japan to oversee the techno-economic aspects of the rig construction. Hiroshima was a citadel of Japanese ship construction before the atomic holocaust that had occurred during the closing stages of World War II. Hiroshima's magic resurgence of three decades symbolized the Japanese determination and entrepreneurship.

Soon, SM Malhotra, SC Upadhyay, SM Kukreja, UA Paul, DS Nandal and many other young and energetic engineers joined the shipyard to learn and identify every nook and cranny of the rig. As massive blocks of steel were being welded to give shape to the jack-up rig, the theatre of action on the Indian shores became more and more frenetic. Simultaneously with the construction of the ship at the Mitsubishi Shipyard in Hiroshima, the French seismic company CGG identified 10 possible locations—all in water depths ranging from 76 to 91 meters. Next, the tide, wave and wind conditions were minutely studied by a newly formed marine survey wing within the company. The seabed survey was the most vexing problem. The clay on the seabed was almost 10 meters thick. Soil strength varied from place to place; in some places, within meters. KS Shankar of the drilling directorate started the well planning. The first well was to be a genuine wildcat. Well planning involved imagination of the sub-surface conditions, downhole pressures, temperatures and the type of formation—all these were anticipated according to the rough geophysical data given by CGG.

Finally, in March 1973, *Samrat* underwent a perfect sea trial in the nearby shores. On 3 April 1973, the drillship set sail from Hiroshima. In brief, it was a tumultuous voyage from Hiroshima to Bombay. *Samrat* moved at snail's pace logging just five knots an hour. It had a 10-day scheduled stopover at Singapore. After 54 days at sea, the crew inhaled the air of India on 25 May 1973. The crew was put on a supply vessel and sent to Mumbai Port. Virender Kumar Verma*, Project Manager of the then newly constituted Mumbai Offshore Project, accorded a warm welcome to the weary passengers. A bonus awaited them. Special sanction had already been taken to provide the crew members with air tickets to reach their homes at the earliest. The poor communication system had caused them a lot of mental anguish and sense of loneliness.

Their journey had ended, and *Samrat's* journey had just begun.

Sagar Samrat Drills its First Well

Meanwhile, a fresh crew to man the *Sagar Samrat* was recruited. Thus in May 1973, about 50 tough men comprising

---

**Verma grew up in Dehra Dun and lived with his siblings at 4, Inder Road.*

roughnecks, derrickmen and roustabouts came on board the newly constructed *Sagar Samrat*.

The first well to be drilled was given the geological name of H–1–1. *Sagar Samrat* and it reached the location by January end 1974. The well was spudded on 3 February and drilling continued without any hitch. About 16 days later at the break of dawn, oil gushed out in great force at 500 PSI (pounds per square inch); its gravity was 43.6 degree API. It kept flowing and was as good as gold. The associated gas was flared since there was no storage facility. Drilling continued up to the target depth of 2,000 meters. Two equally promising oil shows were encountered at 1,400 and 1,600 meters. By a providential coincidence, the drilling was completed on 8 April 1974—just a day before Negi was to retire.

Enter NB Prasad

Starting production from Bombay High became a matter of prime importance. The Petroleum Secretary of the time, PK Dave, asked ONGC to submit a plan for its early production. The incumbent Chairman, BS Negi, was about to retire and development of Bombay High required a high calibre technocrat as his successor.

A special committee comprising PN Haskar, Dr BD Nag Choudhury and Dr Raja Ramanna was constituted to look for a suitable technocrat to head ONGC at that crucial time. The choice finally fell on Nuttaki Bhanu Prasad, a scion of a wealthy family of industrialists from Hyderabad. Prasad had earlier headed the reactor engineering and operations division of Atomic Energy Commission (AEC) where he had won encomiums for the timely commissioning of APSARA and other reactors. For this achievement, Prasad was also awarded the coveted Padma Shri at a relatively young age of 31.

He thus became ONGC's seventh chairman. Prime Minister Indira Gandhi had duly realized the pivotal importance of oil in India's overall economic development. Prasad was therefore given a free hand and a blank cheque to develop the Bombay High field as expeditiously as possible. After two dry wells, the fourth well turned out to be a big gusher. On Thursday 10 April 1975, Prime Minister Indira Gandhi landed on *Samrat* in an IAF helicopter. She climbed up to the rig floor, opened a valve and saw, first hand, the hose pumping oil to the tanker *Jawaharlal Nehru*.

The discovery of Bombay High as a field of high potential had thus become a landmark event, and *Sagar Samrat* a lucky mascot. What was the best way to commemorate that great event? The suggestion by AK Mitra to put *Samrat's* image on a rupee note was readily accepted by Prime Minister Indira Gandhi.

Sagar Samrat has truly lived up to its honorific, the 'Emperor of the Seas'. It has, over its lifespan of 28 years, drilled 130 wells to a total depth of 8,91,336 feet. It has been instrumental in discovering 14 major structures and adding more than three billion metric tonnes of oil and gas reserves. Even in its retirement, *Sagar Samrat* has greatly proved its utility. Until recently, it had been used as living quarters and power backup facility.

CHAPTER 9

The Blowout: Blow by Blow

A blowout is the worst accident that can possibly happen in the hunt for oil. It goes to the credit of ONGC that it responded admirably when there was a blowout on Sagar Vikas.

What happened on that fateful night 36 years ago is a saga of much courage shown by virtually inexperienced men and is worth recalling.

Date:	30 July 1982
Day:	Friday
Time:	9:16 pm
Location:	*Sagar Vikas*, a giant of a structure standing majestically over the SJ Platform, nearly 160 kilometers off Mumbai.
Weather:	High-velocity winds at 30 knots and 15–20 feet sea swells hit the massive legs of the three-leg Japanese-built jack-up.
Characters:	Seventy-four members of an all-Indian crew on board. A few were preparing to go to sleep while others were performing their assigned chores. None of the crew had an inkling of the impending tragedy. Suddenly, the electronic fire alarm system sounded a shrill warning.

Hardly anyone realized the dreadful implications, except perhaps for the men who were at that moment on the well site.

For these unfortunate few, it was the beginning of a nightmare.

Nursing his usual night-cap of strong coffee, sat a young man in a 16th floor wireless room at Maker Towers in Mumbai's predominantly residential locality of Cuffe Parade. He was turning the knobs of various instruments and perhaps looking forward to a restful night.

A flash disturbed the uneasy quiet of a sultry monsoon evening. There was an SOS from aboard the *Sagar Vikas*, 160 kilometers away.

A few miles away, in his plush Malabar Hill apartment, Dr Anil Malhotra, member (offshore), was getting ready for dinner after an unusually hectic day; the shrill ring of his telephone cut into the night's silence. The top brass in the ONGC are accustomed to receiving messages at all odd hours of the day and night. So Dr Malhotra mechanically picked up the receiver. What he heard left him aghast. There was no time to ponder and no time to lose. He made phone calls, one after another, summoning his top aides. Then he drove straight to the Radio Room at Maker Towers.

At *Sagar Vikas*, the first reaction to the blowout was one of disbelief and panic. Naturally, everyone wanted to get away from the jack-up and into the safety of the lifeboats. Fortunately, the panic lasted only a few minutes.

One Man Stood Out

One man stood out among the 74-men crew. He was the crane operator. He took courage literally into his hands as he started lowering his crew mates with the help of a cage (called puggy net) into a waiting anchor-handling supply-tug. Operation Evacuation took less than 30 minutes. The crane operator and another man were the last to get off.

The evacuated crew were transported by two supply vessels to the safety of *Sagar Pragati*.

That Operation Evacuation ended smoothly is evident from the fact that there were no casualties. In a situation like this, in the middle of the rough Arabian Sea, things could have been far worse. Fortunately, there was no stampede and no one fell overboard.

Meanwhile, 1,000 miles away in New Delhi, ONGC Chairman SP Wahi was planning to retire for the night, when he received the dreadful message from Dr Malhotra. He took the first flight on Saturday to Bombay and was at *Sagar Pragati* by 10.30 a.m. *Sagar Pragati* was another jack-up operating about five kilometers from the ill-fated *Sagar Vikas*.

Blowout at Sagar Vikas Drilling Rig/working at Well SJ-5 – Bombay High (30-07-1982) L-R: Harwant Singh Cheema, GGM, offshore operations, Bombay High, Red Adair, the Blowout Specialist, Lovraj Kumar, Secretary Petroleum.
Photo: Moonlite Lotus, Bombay-1

By then *Sagar Pragati* had been turned into a veritable combat headquarter. Dr Malhotra and his senior aides, KC Chandra, SC Mittal, SK Manglik and IL Budhiraja, had flown out there at midnight. HS Cheema, Group General

Manager, took a second helicopter a couple of hours later, K Anjaneyan and Atul Chandra were asked to man the Radio Room in the city. Incidentally, it was the second time in the long offshore operations off Bombay that helicopter sorties were undertaken at night.

The people at combat headquarter deliberated and quickly formulated a strategy to meet the unprecedented situation.

Much before dawn on Saturday, contacts were established with Red Adair, the legendary oil-well fire-fighting expert, in far-off Houston, Texas, USA. Messages were flashed worldwide to find out the availability and the present locations of semi-submersible rigs, fire-fighting vessels and multi-support vessels in order to requisition their services without delay.

Gulf Fleet 46 reached the scene of disaster within four hours and trained its water-jet hoses on *Sagar Vikas*.

Pacific Constructor, a highly efficient multi-support vessel, received the SOS at Mumbai Port, where it had come for refueling. It cruised post-haste to the vicinity of *Sagar Vikas*.

For once, the ONGC (generally shackled like any government undertaking by a plethora of rules and regulation) threw overboard the proverbial red tape and jumped into a frenzy of activity. First, a high-level Control Room was set up and senior executives were put on a round-the-clock vigil in the Wireless Room. It was a virtual state of alert—almost everyone from the chairman down to junior assistants from nearly every discipline was in combat readiness to tackle the emergency. Senior and junior executives rubbed shoulders; the hierarchical barriers were pulled down.

Simultaneously, contingency plans were drawn up to meet any situation arising out of the blowout pending the arrival of Red Adair's trouble-shooters from Houston. In the next few days, orders were placed for the immediate mobilization of a derrick-barge called Hercules at a daily charter rate of $80,000. A semi-submersible Dixilyn Field 95 was chartered for two months in case it became necessary to drill a relief well. A fire-fighting vessel, Flex Service II, was also chartered to augment the existing fire-fighting capability.

Limited enquiries had gone out worldwide for the charter hire of another multi-support vessel, like the Pacific Constructor, to be kept ready for any emergency.

In order to expeditiously take decisions involving crores of rupees, an empowered committee comprising representatives of the Ministries of Petroleum and Chemicals and Finance and that of the ONGC was formed. The committee met every day for hours to clear and approve purchase and charter-hire proposals.

The high drama again shifted to the abandoned *Sagar Vikas*, when the three-day-old blowout turned into a burning inferno on Monday, 2 August at 6.15 a.m. Col SP Wahi flew in again, on that very day, to the scene of the tragedy to oversee the giant fire-fighting operations in which both the Pacific Constructor and the Gulf Fleet 46 were involved.

No Immediate Danger

Luckily, there was no immediate danger to the environment; the threatened pollution—inevitable in such situations—did not materialize. Meanwhile, ONGC personnel were keeping their fingers crossed. When three of the Red Adair fire-fighting daredevils finally reached Mumbai, they were whisked straight to the scene.

The experts probed into the possible causes of the blowout. Whatever appeared in the press, was at best, speculative. Human error is likely to be a cause: most blowouts or, for that matter, other accidents, occur because of this factor.

That the ONGC personnel, under the stewardship of Col Wahi, rose to the occasion as never before was obvious. Not many among the ONGC's top brass then had encountered a blowout even on land. To have this accident happen on the high seas was something that was completely unprecedented—something which could have left much more experienced bunch of people in a virtual state of panic. The fact that the ONGC management did not lose its cool and calmly went about Operation Evacuation should stand to its credit.

High praise has come for the management from an unexpected source; the ONGC's Association of Scientific and Technical Officers. ASTO—at times quick to find fault—

on this occasion, patted the management for 'handling the situation with utmost expediency'.

According to its local president, RS Ghai, 'all action, from fighting the fire to the welfare measures, was planned within a very short time and no oil company in the world could claim such a quick action, as taken by the ONGC.' ASTO also put on record its sincere appreciation of the top management in general, and Col Wahi and Dr Malhotra in particular for providing excellent leadership and for working shoulder to shoulder with other employees in the face of dire peril.

And now a team led by the legendary Paul Neale, Red Adair, has drawn up, in consultation with the ONGC, a detailed plan to cap and kill the stricken well SJ-5. Derrick barge Hercules, which will be used as the principal working platform for the operation, has reached the location and is ready to start Operation Capping as soon as the weather permits. Dixilyn Field 95—a semi-submersible rig—is also in Bombay High waiting to drill a relief well, should it become necessary.

A specially designed and fabricated well-head has been flown to Bombay from Singapore, after it was thoroughly tested by the ONGC engineers and a Red Adair team member. All other equipment needed for the task was rapidly assembled at the site.

Postscript: On the third day, the abandoned *Sagar Vikas* exploded into flames. The naval fire-fighting ships controlled the blaze from spreading.

CHAPTER 10

The Two Stalwarts

AMN Ghosh
The First and Foremost

*A*ustin *Manindra Nath Ghosh was the first among the equals. He epitomized the power of sheer determination. He was the superintending geologist at the GSI and enjoyed the distinction of being the first director of ONGC. He spent the last four years of his life in building ONGC brick-by-brick, even though many sceptics had initially dismissed it as a pipedream.*

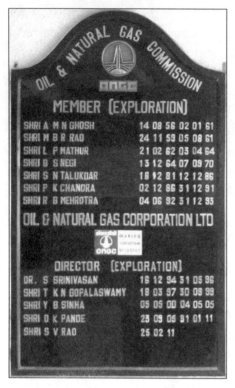

When Malaviya zeroed in on Ghosh to head the ONGC directorate, he would attribute the latter's choice to his impeccable reputation at GSI. A trait they shared was reposing faith in local talent. Ghosh inspired a generation of young pioneers. He evoked in equal measure fear, respect and loyalty. Ghosh was truly a field geologist nonpareil.

Born on 14 June 1902, Ghosh grew up in Calcutta, and graduated in geology from Presidency College. He joined the ranks of field geologists in GSI in 1924.

By 1928, he was on his way to the University of London to pursue higher studies where he earned a first class master's degree. His brilliance brought him an associateship at the Royal College of Sciences.

Having been chosen by Malaviya to lay a strong foundation for the nascent directorate, he put all his experience to work. Brought up in the British tradition, he would enforce discipline with an iron hand; he demanded perfection in everything, and had a special liking for hard workers. In those early days, life was hectic. Ghosh would leave office very late at night, sometimes at 11. His moments of great triumph were the oil discoveries in Cambay and Ankleshwar. But the effort took its toll. He suffered a heart attack on a train as he was on his way from Cambay to Dehra Dun; he never recovered. Ghosh died on 2 January 1961; he was only 59. In a rare gesture, the Government of India issued a black-bordered notification after his death: 'On his passing away, India has lost an able and trusted public servant who served his country with distinction in the geological field... the credit of achieving the results of the Oil and Natural Gas Commission's work in record time goes to him...he had the gift of organization and of quick and sound judgement. He will long be remembered for his meritorious service to the cause of oil geology of India'.

AMN Ghosh Auditorium

To commemorate him ONGC named its spacious auditorium in KDMIPE after him. In a way, KDMIPE is known to the ordinary residents of Dehra Dun more for its top-of-the class auditorium than for its sterling contribution in the field of research and development in the E & P sectors of the petroleum industry.

MBR Rao
An Outstanding Geoscientist

Though he was a geologist by background, Mandagere Bhardwaj Ramachandra Rao, in the course of a distinguished career, had also acquired expertise in the science of geophysics. In a way, it was fortuitous that Rao was deputed for geophysical training to USA, the UK and Canada in 1947-48. Thus, he became one of the few geoscientists with equal felicity in geology and geophysics.

Rao was born on 5 August 1906, in a village called Mandagere in the Mandya district of, what is now, Karnataka. At the age of 20, he secured a bachelor's degree in science with geology as major. Rao's first job was with the Mysore Geological Department. He worked hard, and learnt fast. In the midst of strenuous fieldwork, Rao managed time to pursue his studies, and obtain an M.Sc degree in 1933 from Mysore University, with a first class, and a gold medal.

But the story of how Rao got involved with geophysics is interesting. In 1937, the Kolar gold mining industry secured the services of one AB Broghton Edge for investigating gold bearing quartz veins; Rao volunteered to work with his party. That association brought out in full measure the geophysicist in Rao. Soon, he was the architect of the geophysical section of the Mysore Geological Department.

That was a few years before the GSI was to set up its own geophysical wing. No wonder, MBR Rao will always be known as the Father of Indian Geophysics.

On his return from the US in 1949, Rao was asked to head the newly formed geophysical wing at GSI. The unassuming scientist was only 43. Geophysical investigations for oil in Cambay and Kaveri basins in the pre-ONGC days were among his achievements at the GSI.

At 51, Rao was made the Director of Geophysics in ONGC. His task was to provide dynamic leadership in the planning and execution of magnetic gravity, seismic and electrologging operations all over the country. When ONGC became a statutory body in 1959, Rao was elevated to the rank of its member (Technical and Administration).

In his long professional career, there have been many milestones; he was a father figure to scores of young geoscientists. Rao's professional credentials were impeccable. He was large-hearted, too. Simplicity and modesty were his credos.

He was a prolific writer on geophysical investigations; over 65 published papers bore testimony to his mastery over his pet subject. His much acclaimed book *Outlines of Geophysical Prospecting*, published in 1975, long after he had laid down his tools as a practicing exploration geophysicist, demonstrated his abiding interest.

He was a man for all seasons; as much at home among members of geological and seismic field parties as he was in the company of Indian and foreign scientists. Nehru, too, began to like this scholarly geoscientist. Once, when the prime minister wanted someone to address the Parliament on the fundamentals of oil exploration and to underline its importance in India's economic development and self-reliance, his choice was Rao.

No wonder, Nehru endearingly gave him the sobriquet, Oil Man. For his meritorious and distinguished services to the country, MBR was awarded the Padma Bhushan in 1972.

CHAPTER 11

The Chairmen

Leslie James Johnson

(May 1966–September 1970)

"I was brought up to stand by my convictions. I have always been able to sleep content in the knowledge that I am a poor, rich man." LJ Johnson

This was Mr Johnson's creed, and he had lived by it all of his life.

When ONGC's C&MD in 2001, Subir Raha, had urged his *parivar* of 40,000-odd members to inculcate amongst themselves the absolute qualities of honesty and integrity in all their manifestations, he should have

also advised them to adopt Leslie James Johnson as their role model.

Johnson, by general consensus, was one of the most popular chairmen of ONGC. He remained at its helm for four years from 1966 to 1970 and left at the end of his tenure an indelible legacy of honesty, integrity and simplicity. He was, indeed, a legend and his contribution will be long remembered.

In fact, he was the only bigwig I have known who would enter in the log book of the staff car his commuting from his Rajpur home to Tel Bhawan and back as private journeys and paid for the same from his pocket. 'Johnson was easily accessible and scrupulously honest,' says SN Talukdar, an ONGC veteran. Even though he was new to the nitty-gritty of the oil business, he had quickly picked up its rudiments and had also acquired a certain degree of sophistication to the extent that he could speak in the lingua of technocrats and became sharp enough to grasp a given problem and focus on it.

Johnson was an embodiment of integrity—personal, professional and .managerial. His ingrained honesty and above board behaviour had impressed one and all.

He formally joined ONGC as Chairman on 8 September 1966, after a four-month stint in a stop-gap arrangement during the absence of his predecessor, Mr A. Zaman; both Zaman and Johnson were from the ICS cadre. In the preceding years, the state of the health of ONGC had gone from bad to worse. Things had come to such a pass that the stipulated drilling and production targets were given a go by. Drilling meterage had plummeted to 23 per cent of its target in the first seven months of 1996-97. Johnson was extremely concerned at that all-pervasive tardiness and indiscipline.

Johnson First Tackled Lethargy

The first step he took was to attack the lethargy that had gripped Tel Bhawan, which was then the nerve centre of ONGC. The entire top brass was based at Dehra Dun and Johnson soon closeted with his senior advisors to arrest the slide and bring ONGC back to health. Though a minor step to begin with, a siren system was introduced that blared at 10 a.m. and 5 p.m. to announce the official working hours. That practice continues even today, as a futile and ineffectual ritual. Names of the latecomers were recorded in a register and the staff was not allowed to leave the office complex during the prescribed working hours. This practice did bring about some semblance of discipline. But more serious and complex a problem was to enforce discipline and accountability in the projects located in Gujarat in the west, and Assam in east India. Absence of accountability then, as today, was considered the main culprit for its falling performance. Another was the utter lack of coordination among the various branches. Each discipline then tended to become a law unto itself.

Johnson's first innovative step was to set up a control room in the basement of the three-storeyed administrative building at Tel Bhawan. Similar control rooms were also set up in the regions for daily monitoring of the day's work. A Daily Progress Report (called DPR) was received from each project either by telegram or wireless giving out the figures of the meterage drilled and oil and gas produced that day. These reports also mentioned any problems faced and confronted and solutions, if any, arrived at. For a solution to more complex and difficult breakdowns or shutdowns, advice was promptly sent from Dehra Dun.

Thus, by establishing a network of control rooms at the headquarters and at the work centres, ONGC was able to monitor the daily activities throughout the country and bring about an all-round improvement in the drilling and production performances. In a way, this control room concept soon became a model for other undertakings that sent some of their senior executives to study the system. IAS probationers from Mussoorie, too, put Tel Bhawan on their annual *Bharat Darshan Yatra*, itinerary.

Monetary Incentives Introduced

Monetary incentives were also introduced for drilling, production and other crews that met or exceeded their given targets. Johnson also started the practice of sending individual letters of appreciation to those who performed well enough. Incidentally, Raha too used to compliment asset managers who had achieved 100 per cent plus production targets.

A unique feature of the daily control room meetings was that Mr Johnson attended it every day, punctually at 4 p.m. along with other heads of departments and reviewed the performance reports received from various projects. It was a stocktaking, so the daily activity analysis review and deliberations at these meetings were short, serious and productive. Hardly any meeting lasted more than an hour.

Though the setting up of the control room was Mr Johnson's idea, it was a team led by Mr MB Deshmukh, a friend of mine who actually conceptualized it. The other members of this team were Messrs IL Budhiraja (he later became a director in GAIL and once headed the oil and gas division of Reliance Industries), S Murthy, ML Dora (he is involved with the SD School (Bannu) at Race Course as a manager) and VC Singhal. All the members of this team were given two advance increments for the excellent services rendered.

Some Other Notable Achievements

Some of the major achievements of Johnson were:
- The revision of pay-scales of officers on the eve of demitting his office, despite stiff opposition from the representative of the ministry on the board of the Commission.
- Officers concerned were asked to submit a working paper summarizing the subject instead of writing lengthy notes when submitting a file.
- A small beginning was made during his tenure in offshore drilling with a

locally fabricated small platform at Aliabet in the Gulf of Cambay near Bhavnagar. Prime Minister Indira Gandhi spudded the well in March 1970. It was later abandoned as no reserves of commercial quantity were found. Yet, a small step was taken towards the subsequent discovery of Bombay High.

Another first introduced by Johnson was the job numbering scheme with a view to controlling the inventory. The practice continues even today but one must thank Johnson for his pioneering innovation.

In order to enforce discipline and ensure proper working ambience, Johnson used to make rounds of Tel Bhawan during the lunch break.

He was zealously assisted in his task by Chief of Administration Brig SC Vyas whose very sight would send the loitering employees scurrying to their seats.

Johnson did not believe in all work and no play. He rarely overstayed in office and in his spare time indulged in hobbies such like photography, writing and playing the piano. He was a painter of no mean calibre and his forte was painting lampshades and landscapes especially of mountains in oil paints. On Sundays and other holidays Johnson accompanied by his wife Vendla, would go visiting the nearby mountains and forests in order to satiate his appetite for painting and photography. Unlike the bosses of today, he would try to make use of the leave he deservedly earned.

And Now the Beginning

To begin at the beginning; not many people today would recall that Johnson was born in Mussoorie in September 1914 and had had his schooling at the St. George's College.

His father, James Henry Johnson, was a surveyor and later turned a journalist and published *The Mussoorie Times*. He had also owned a printing press and a bookshop-cum-library.

He sent his son Leslie to Lahore for higher education where he studied at its iconic Government College. Leslie secured bachelor's and master's degrees in English. After his selection to the ICS, Leslie was sent to New Oxford College, England for his ICS training.

From 1939 onwards he held, with distinction, numerous posts, mostly in the United and Central Provinces, before coming on deputation to Delhi. Incidentally, he was the first Chief Secretary of Delhi and thus attracted the attention of Mr Mehr Chand Khanna, Minister for Relief and Rehabilitation in Nehru's cabinet. Johnson simultaneously held three important posts, viz., (i) Joint Secretary, (ii) Chief Settlement Commissioner and (iii) Custodian General of India. By his pleasing disposition, hard work and sincerity of purpose, Johnson had become the blue-eyed boy of the minister, who himself was a refugee from Pakistan.

His Paintings Bore a Professional Stamp

Johnson's paintings bore a professional stamp. He had held one-man painting exhibitions in New Delhi and Mumbai, at which most of his paintings were snapped up by the connoisseur. Johnson was gracious enough to invite me to his Delhi exhibition held at All India Fine Arts and Crafts Society Auditorium at Rafi Marg. I invited Mrs and Mr Johnson and others to lunch at the Marina Hotel, Connaught Place, though I could then hardly afford the cost, but the hotel owner, having known me from earlier days, gave me a hefty discount.

Life After Retirement

Johnson lived in Dehra Dun's Rajpur suburb after his retirement, where he had bought a bungalow. That property however, caused some avoidable headache. He got involved in a protracted litigation with the State Government over the matter of surplus land under the Urban Land Ceiling Act. Though Johnson eventually won the case at Allahabad High Court, the tension of litigation had sapped his natural enthusiasm and zest for life. Mr Johnson then decided to settle in Bangalore, where his younger sibling, Kenneth, had settled after his retirement as the Chief Commissioner of income tax.

This is the story of an ICS officer who did not assume any airs and was utterly unassuming. What really prompted me to write this story in February 2002 is the fact that a couple of months before, I received a long letter from Johnson. Its contents deserved to be reproduced and should have been of interest to those who had known or heard of him, and should also be a source of inspiration to the present generation of ONGC fraternity. It is unfortunate that I have misplaced that letter and hence am unable to share its contents with the readers.

Though ailing and lonesome, with impaired vision, in 2002, Johnson had not lost interest in the things he loved. He looked forward to the publication of his memoirs and I sincerely pray he will live to see those.

What kind of tribute could ONGC pay to one of its most popular chairmen? If I were in the shoes of the current C & MD, I would hold a meeting with the board of directors of ONGC, in the near future at Bangalore, provided Mr Johnson is healthy enough to receive the board directors and others at his Whitefield home. People like Dr. Hari Narain, SN Talukdar and others, who worked with Mr Johnson, could also be invited. This should, indeed, be a fitting and touching tribute to a distinguished chairman.

Balwant Singh Negi

(September 1970–April 1974)

BS Negi was thoroughly professional and professionally thorough. However, being a geoscientist of repute himself, he would often differ with senior scientists on the interpretation of some specific field data, and arguments would then carry on almost till midnight.

Negi incidentally was the first ONGC insider to have been elevated to the coveted post of its chairman. A geophysicist from the stable of GSI, he was widely known for his indecisiveness. 'Negi was a stickler for rules and regulations and lacked the aggressive drive of leadership and qualities of effective man management so very essential in giving proper direction to a vibrant organization', wrote Iqbal Farooqi in his book *The Story of ONGC*.

However, on the positive side, it needs to be stressed that the exploration and development of Bombay High was undertaken during Mr Negi's tenure as member (Exploration) when Johnson was the chairman. Negi should also be given the credit for discovering Bombay High and for the purchase of ONGC's first jack-up rig *Sagar Samrat* that gave a big impetus to offshore exploration.

I was the first time that ONGC was required to make an investment of ₹12.7 crores that was, at that time, a huge investment, and it needed a lot of guts to take a call on that. However, it was altogether a different Negi who then showed uncharacteristic resoluteness and courage in handling the delicate and complex negotiations with Mitsubishi. Thus an order was placed for a self propelled jack-up rig in February 1971. The rig arrived in Bombay High on 31 January 1974.

Three weeks later on 19 February, oil was discovered in a limestone reservoir. The rest is history.

Negi was also among the first few ONGCians to have acquired a car when he joined the ranks of Ambassador owners. It was black in colour with UPS 5021 as its registration number; almost everyone in ONGC would remember that number. That was Negi's first and only purchase of a car; he drove that car for over 40 years until his demise. Even today the old faithful car quietly sits in a locked garage at Negi's 30A Rajpur Road residence.

NB Prasad: A Hyderabad Technocrat

(April 1974–September 1978)

It was, however, NB Prasad, a Hyderabad technocrat and industrialist, who was solely instrumental in stepping up the exploration and production activity in Bombay High, making it the most prolific oilfield in the country. Prasad also concentrated more on the development of offshore fields, introducing latest western technologies while sadly ignoring onshore areas which until then were ONGC's bread and butter.

A popular initiative by Prasad was introduction of generous travelling and daily allowances (TA and DA). Until then, ONGC personnel were paid niggardly TA and DA similar to those being paid to the officers and employees of the Central Government. With one stroke, he substantially upgraded those allowances and permitted touring

ONGC officers to stay in star hotels depending upon their individual entitlement. Thus, overnight, officers of the rank of general managers and deputy general managers started staying at five-star and four-star hotels without any direct payment. In lieu of this luxurious accommodation and sumptuous meals, a very nominal amount was deducted from their daily allowance. Even junior officers were asked to stay in hotels of lower star ratings. These travelling perks were much better than those given by most private companies and at par with what was then being given by top Indian companies.

Special Offshore Allowances

Another praiseworthy measure was the payment of special allowance to personnel operating on offshore installations. They worked on the basis of 14-day on and off. They would return at the end of their shift to their home base, for which ONGC paid the to and fro rail fare by the applicable class. That way Prasad greatly softened the effect of sea-loneliness and also allowed the offshore personnel to spend two weeks every month with their families.

Prasad also gave a new chic décor to the various offices of ONGC. Until then, most offices wore a drab and dreary look. He got those offices totally renovated. His own office in the Bank of Baroda building in New Delhi bore testimony to his exquisite taste and elegance. Also, all the offices in Mumbai were decorated in consonance with the latest trends in office interiors. The multistorey building in Mumbai's Bandra, Vasudhara Bhavan that today houses most of the offices of ONGC's Mumbai Regional Business Centre, was conceived, designed and constructed during the tenure of Prasad though its completion, interiors and inauguration were done by Wahi.

Prasad also hired a large number of spacious flats in Cuffe Parade, around the Colaba and Bandra localities in Mumbai for senior officers with hefty furnishing allowances. He also paid refundable deposits of as much as 20 lakhs to landlords.

Generous Perks

The perks available at that time to ONGC personnel were unheard of even in most generous private companies. He also put at the disposal of his senior officers (chief engineers and above) a rental car for most of the day and part of the night. It is, however, debatable if that pampering helped evoke a commensurate response by way of additional dedication and commitment to their duty from ONGC officers. On the contrary, some of them started behaving like spoiled brats and proved themselves unworthy of that largesse.

Some of the senior officers proved themselves undeserving recipients of five-star hotel facilities by stealing fine China crockery and sterling silver cutlery from their hotel rooms. The Oberoi kept designer robes in bathrooms with a notice that guests are most welcome to buy one for ₹250; I bought one. But a group of general manager just took away the robe without batting an eyelid.

Prasad too, had his own idiosyncrasies. Once on a flight, he gave an appointment offer in ONGC on an empty cigarette pack to a fellow passenger, and that offer was duly honoured.

Col SP Wahi was his Own Man

(October 1981–December 1989)

In the history of India's public sector enterprises, there have not been many managers like Col SP Wahi.

His was a long odyssey that commenced in 1943 from an obscure town in what is now Pakistan. Journeying through myriad educational and professional institutions, he finally reached the Banaras Hindu University where he earned an engineering degree with distinction.

The army was his next stop; he was commissioned in the Corp of EME in December 1950. In his 22-year-long  and varied career in the army, Col Wahi acquired many new skills and technologies. More importantly, it was in the army that he imbibed those sterling qualities of leadership that later came in handy in the corporate world; it was there that he learned the meaning of self-respect and the importance of how to walk with one's head high, and all that added another dimension to his charismatic persona that remained his hallmark throughout his multifaceted career.

It was in the last lap of his army career that Col Wahi had his first taste of the public sector in November 1969 when he was sent on a short deputation to the Bokaro Steel Plant which was still under construction. That short deputation lasted nearly five years, taking him to the Soviet Union on numerous occasions in order to ensure the timely completion of the steel plant. That was the beginning of Wahi's second innings. Bharat Heavy Electricals Ltd and the Cement Corporation of India were the other public sector undertakings where

Col Wahi left his indelible stamp. It was, however, at ONGC that Col Wahi earned much name and fame and created a unique niche for himself that only a very few of his successors were to match.

My First Meeting with Col Wahi

My first meeting with Col Wahi happened by sheer accident one summer day in 1981. I had an appointment with a senior ONGC executive at his plush office in Dehra Dun. As I gently pushed his slightly ajar door, I noticed a well-dressed gentleman sitting there. Noticing my hesitation, the officer said, 'Come in, come in'. Introducing the visitor, the officer said, 'Meet Col SP Wahi, the future Chairman of ONGC'. His reputation as a dynamic corporate honcho at BHEL in the nearby Haridwar plant and the Cement Corporation of India had already preceded him. A broad forehead rested atop an intense face and sparkling eyes; long sideburns and a handlebar moustache stood out. He introduced me as the chairman of a company representing several foreign oilfield equipment manufacturers in India, and added, in passing, that I was ONGC's first Public Relations Officer. Col Wahi stood up, firmly shook my hand and gave me an intent look as if to appraise me. After exchanging a few courtesies, Col Wahi left.

Wahi had joined ONGC as Officer on Special Duty nearly four months prior to formally taking over in October 1981 as its 9th chairman. He productively spent those four months in learning about the various facets of the complex oil industry. He visited as many laboratories and as many work centres as possible and picked the brains of young and old engineers, scientists, drillers and the lot. Much, much later, he told me, 'Kanwar, learning is a lifelong process and one is never too old to learn'. It was that short stint as a student that helped Col Wahi untie some of the knotty and complex issues that ONGC faced then. Many of the innovative practices that he introduced at that time had stood the test of time.

Fortuitously, Col Wahi was the right choice as ONGC's head honcho at that time. NB Prasad in his four-year tenure as ONGC's Chairman had earlier put the prolific Bombay High field on even keel. Wahi gave a bigger boost to the offshore operations virtually doubling the production by the time his tenure ended. His achievements very often featured in the evening news bulletins on Doordarshan that was then only TV channel.

Leading from the Front

Wahi was known for his hands-on approach and believed in leading from the front. Incidentally, *Leading from the Front: From Army to Corporate World* is also the title of his memoir that received rave reviews. I have had the rare privilege of watching from the sidelines many such acts that Col Wahi had performed in the course of his long tenure with ONGC. Its personnel had been stagnating for years. Wahi did away with the stagnation by introducing time-bound promotions. With just one stroke, he boosted their morale and injected a new sense of enthusiasm in them.

However, the most courageous was his prompt and effective tackling of the disastrous blowout on the jack-up *Sagar Vikas* on 30 July 1982. Col Wahi was then in New Delhi and was planning to retire for the night when he received a dreadful message from Dr Anil Malhotra, the member in-charge of offshore operations. Without thinking twice, he took the first flight to Bombay the following morning, and by breakfast was at *Sagar Pragati*, another Jack-up that then operated just about five kilometers away from the ill-fated *Sagar Vikas*. His troubleshooting ability was at its best that day. In no time, a contact was established with the legendary oil-well fire-fighting expert Red Adair in far-off Houston, Texas. Messages were also flashed worldwide to find out the availability and current locations of semi-submersible rigs, fire-fighting vessels and multi-support vessels so that their services could be acquired without any delay. The rest is history and well documented in an earlier chapter.

The blowout had instantly become big news and reporters vied with one another in order to discover scoops. Kumud C Khanna, the late venerated editor of *The Illustrated Weekly of India* called me. 'Raj, you are the only person who can give me a write up on *Sagar Vikas* in 24 hours'. I was then full-time in business and had not done any significant writing over the last 10 years or so. However, I did not wish to disappoint my friend who had placed so much trust in my ability. Mobile phones were then unheard of. Somehow, I managed to station myself at the ONGC Radio Room in Maker Towers in Cuff Parade and was able to piece together a credible sequence of events leading to the disastrous blowout and its aftermath. My article under the heading *'Sagar Vikas Blowout – a blow by blow account'* appeared the following week and was greatly appreciated for its accuracy and technical finesse.

The Woman Behind Wahi

Behind every successful man, it is said, there is a woman. It was Shobhana, his wife of 59 years, who played a great supporting role in his success. Wahis' bungalow in the Tel Bhawan campus in Dehra Dun would become an open house on *Diwali*. In a unique practice, Col Wahi and wife Shobhana would give a return packet of sweets to all those who came to wish them a happy *Diwali*.

On one such occasion, my wife and I individually

received a packet each. In fact, a part of the credit of Wahi's immense popularity goes to Shobhana. In no time, she had become friendly with the wives of

ONGCians and freely interacted with them. It was at her initiative that a women's polytechnic was set up in Dehra Dun on 27 June 1987 which offered a variety of courses in interior design and decoration, textile design, fashion design, modern office management and secretarial practice, computer applications, garment technology and so on.

During the eight years, Col Wahi remained ONGC's Chairman, my relations with him remained broadly formal, though warm. I greatly respected him for his uprightness and the dignity with which he conducted himself. We shared courtesies by sending greeting cards. Wahi was courteous to a fault and punctilious in keeping appointments. Once when I visited him at his Delhi office with prior appointment, even though another visitor was sitting with him at that time, he came out to speak with me, apologizing at the same time. In the 1970s and 1980s, my business flourished not because of any favours bestowed or concessions given but because of my professional business approach. We then represented some of the high-profile American companies and got substantial orders on pure merit. I could of course have cultivated closer relations with Wahi, but didn't as it was my wont.

Prestigious URJA Award

Col Wahi had received a standing ovation in March 2015 when India's Finance Minister Arun Jaitely presented him with the prestigious URJA Award for his outstanding contribution to the Indian oil and gas industry. He had been the recipient of numerous awards in his long and distinguished career including the coveted Padma Bhushan in 1988. Though he is a year older than me, he remained active in his numerous voluntary activities.

Our relationship turned into friendship after he retired. In particular, we became closer when I met him on more than a couple of occasions during the writing of the official history of ONGC. In the recent years, my respect for him has gone up several notches. He too, I dare believe, has discovered many of my hitherto latent talents such as my intellectual grasp and kind heart. I had also become very friendly with his older brother, the late OP Wahi, who then managed Dehra Dun's Sri Aurobindo Ashram, and his older sister Pushpa Mehta, a great social worker; I greatly admired her for her compassion and kindness. Our last meeting took place in September 2015 when Col Wahi came to Dehra Dun as a grief-stricken brother on the sudden demise of Mrs Mehta. I sat with him for a long time holding his hand and mumbling meaningless words of empathy and consolation.

PK Chandra: A Brilliant Geologist

(December 1989–June 1990)

*P*K *Chandra belonged to the 1956 batch of some of the brilliant geologists who had then joined the nascent ONGC. Happily, most of those geologists, like Chandra, were Bengalis and as such shared mutual bonhomie.*

One of the most crucial jobs entrusted to Chandra and his fellow neo-geologists was to undertake the geological mapping of sedimentary basins. It was easier said than done. The area to be explored was scattered, expansively wide and generally inhospitable. However, it redounded to the credit of those young geologists that they happily and willingly faced the hazards of those barren deserts and harsh mountains and successfully performed the given tasks.

The geological field parties in the state of Assam faced

Chandra with Prof. Nikolay Zapivalov, the leader of the Russian delegation to PETROTECH India

their own peculiar problems. Chandra reminisces seeing a red cloth tied to a tree when doing field work in the jungles of Silchar. The locals were apprehensive. But the work continued. A group of insurgents from across the border confronted the party, mistaking their look for something ominous. The Sola hat and the thick belts, which resembled bullet pouches, caused them concern. Chandra calmly explained the purpose of their work; the seismic parties used to carry large quantities of explosives. Those were never stolen. People had come to realize and appreciate the vital importance of their work. The scientists were there to add value to their wealth.

He continued to climb the hierarchical ladder in ONGC until he virtually reached the top as the officiating chairman. However, Chandra felt somewhat handicapped because of its officiating status. Yet, he tried his best to meet, within the given limitations, the exacting challenges of his job.

LL Bhandari: A Complete Geologist

(October 1992–January 1993)

*L*axmi Lal Bhandari was quietly efficient. He was *punctilious to a fault and calmly undertook his responsibilities without any hassles.*

When oil was discovered in Bombay High, Bhandari meticulously double checked every detail about that discovery

before sending good tidings to Chairman Negi. As was his wont, Negi was sceptical and asked Bhandari if the oil find would compare with that of Ankleshwar.

He was somewhat conservative when he said that the offshore find was twice the size of Ankleshwar. His estimate was widely off the mark. As more and more wells were drilled, the Bombay discovery turned out to be a gold mine.

He was one of the most promising geologists in the 1956 batch of young men. In his lifelong career in ONGC, he had held many an important assignment reaching the highest peak on 30 September 1992 as the Chairman-in-Charge. His predecessor SL Khosla had revised pay scales and it was left to Bhandari to implement those retrospectively from 1987.

He was, in a way, a complete geologist. He was the project manager in 1974 in Bombay, and was among the few lucky ones to have witnessed the first oil strike on 19 February 1974. He was given the *Shiromani* award by the President in 1986 'for having risen to one of the highest positions in ONGC by virtue of hard work, sincerity and dedication, for his matchless contribution in the field of exploration for Oil and Gas in the country'.

CHAPTER 12

Chairmen & Managing Directors

SK Manglik

(January 1993–April 1995)

In his eventful career spanning 36 years, Sushil Kumar Manglik has been an important part of ONGC's phenomenal growth. With a graduation degree in mechanical engineering from the Benaras Hindu University, he had joined ONGC in 1958.

He was head of the production operations at Ankleshwar, Gujarat in 1962. It was during his tenure that production started from ONGC oil-fields in Assam and the supply of oil to Guwahati Refinery commenced. He was also instrumental in commissioning the pipeline network for supply of crude to Baroda Refinery.

He had also been a pioneer in offshore operations and was responsible for the operation of the first ONGC owned jack-up rig *Sagar Samrat* and the chartered jack-up rig Shanendoah in Bombay Offshore.

Not only did he supervise the design, construction and commissioning of the first Cryogenic LPG Recovery Plant at

Uran, but he was also responsible for the construction of the first Gas Sweetening Complex at Hazira in Gujarat.

During his tenure as the Regional Director of Central Region Business Centre, he was instrumental in bringing about a dramatic improvement in its operations. Tripura was upgraded to a category-I basin and the first revenue was earned by the region through gas sales. The first offshore well in the central region was spudded in the Calcutta offshore area during his tenure.

He joined the ONGC Board as member (Technical) in July 1987. A total of seven process platforms and 36 well platforms were constructed and installed during his tenure. Projects such as Neelam, L-III infill, L-II development and R-15 A Phase-I with a combined potential to contribute about 9 MMT were initiated. Communications set-up in ONGC was totally modernized. Environment, safety, indigenization and conservation of energy received great thrust and several initiatives were taken in those areas.

He held many important positions besides being CMD, ONGC. He was President, Institute of Mechanical Engineers (India), member, Technology Information Forecasting and Assessment Council, Department of Science and Technology, Governor and Chairman of Board of Governors of the ONGC Schlumberger Wireline Research Centre amongst other things.

Manglik won several awards during his illustrious career in ONGC including the *First Rajiv Gandhi Memorial National Award* in 1991 and *Udyog Gaurav,* 1992 and *Udyog Rattan* in 1993 for his distinguished contribution towards the industrial development of the country.

It was by sheer dent of his hard work and competence that he rose to occupy the top position in ONGC. It was during his tenure that ONGC had assumed its new avatar of a corporate entity by shedding the *chola* of a statutory undertaking. That this corporate transformation went through smoothly was, in no small measure, due to his stewardship.

प्रारूप एक
Form 1
निगमन का प्रमाण-पत्र
Certificate of Incorporation

सं० __55-54155__ .... शक .... 19 __15__ ....
No. __55-54155__ .... of ...... 19 __93-94__ ....

मैं एतद् द्वारा प्रमाणित करता हूं कि आज __ऑयल एण्ड नेचुरल गैस__ __कारपोरेशन लिमिटेड__

कम्पनी अधिनियम 1956 (1956 का 1) के प्रधीन निगमित की गई है और यह कम्पनी परिसीमित है ।

I hereby certify that __OIL AND NATURAL GAS__ __CORPORATION LIMITED__

is this day incorporated under the Companies Act, 1956 (No. 1 of 1956) and that the Company is Limited.

मेरे हस्ताक्षर से आज ता० __2 आषाढ़, 1915__ को दिया गया ।

Given under my hand at __NEW DELHI__ this __TWENTY THIRD__

day of __JUNE__ One thousand nine hundred and NINETY __THREE__

। एच. एस. शर्मा ।
अतर   कम्पनी रजिस्ट्रार
दिल्ली एवं हरियाणा
(H.S. SHARMA)
ADDL. Registrar of Companies
DELHI & HARYANA

Apart from BS Negi, who had cut his professional teeth with GSI and remained ONGC Chairman for five years, albeit in officiating capacity, the other three, namely, Manglik, Chandra and Bhandari too had their baptism in ONGC and were truly the sons of the soil.

Bikash C Bora
India's Most Versatile Oilman

(August 1995–April 2001)

Digboi in Assam was India's first oilfield discovered in 1890 by Assam Railways and Trading Company, and later transferred to the erstwhile Assam Oil Company. And for the following 66 years until the birth of ONGC in 1956, Assam remained the only oil producing province in the country, and its residents then dominated the Indian petroleum scene. However, it then took ONGC—India's first public sector oil major—and the Central Government 39 years before an Assamese native could be appointed as its head honcho.

It was thus that Bikash Chandra Bora became ONGC's Chairman-cum-Managing Director on 23 August 1995. He was 54. Bora still remains the lone Assamese to have had the distinction of being ONGC's Chairman. The only other Assamese was AK Hazarika, who briefly officiated as ONGC's CMD in the interregnum between the retirement of  RS Sharma and the formal appointment of Sudhir Vasudeva.

Bora had then brought to his office 38 years of rich experience in the E & P areas of the petroleum industry. A mechanical engineering graduate from Benaras Hindu University, Bora joined Oil India Ltd in 1962. For the following 20 years, Bora steadily rose in the Oil India hierarchy, winning accolades both in India and abroad. In 1982, Bora took up a challenging three-year stint as the chief engineer of an

American oil company operating in Peru. He returned to
Oil India Ltd. in 1985 and within seven years became its CMD
in 1992.

ONGC stood at a crossroads in 1995. With the
introduction of New Exploration Licencing Policy (NELP) and
the onslaught of liberalization and globalization, ONGC's
monopolistic status faced new challenges. The upstream
petroleum industry in India that was until then the exclusive
preserve of ONGC had been thrown open to multinational
oil companies as also to large private companies in India.
International bids were invited for scores of oil and gas
blocks under NELP, and ONGC also stood in the queue, like
any other bidder. It was at that juncture that Bora took over
the reins of ONGC and courageously faced the new global
challenges emerging successful through this baptism of fire
in globalization.

If the domestic industry then faced the challenge of the
multinational companies entering India's upstream sector,
its flip side was it also got a level playing field in making its
own forays with equal ease into foreign markets. Thus ONGC
Videsh Ltd (OVL), under Bora's chairmanship extended
its wings to international territories, hitherto virgin and
somewhat daunting for Indian entities such as ONGC. With
Atul Chandra as his second-in-command, Bora aggressively
pursued acquisition of promising and high-potential acreages
and oil or gas blocks in other countries, notably Vietnam and
some of the erstwhile Soviet republics.

International Practices

Bora had then realized that it was absolutely necessary to bring
ONGC's practices at par with international oil companies in
the matter of technical excellence, decision-making and cost
effectiveness. With that end in view, he brought to the table
the global consultants McKinsey, and set in motion in 1999

an Organization Transformation Project, redefining the new objectives and the strategic direction of the organization. It was during Bora's tenure that modern IT systems in finance, material management, HRD, exploration and production were introduced.

Bora had also given equal attention to streamlining the revenue-earning operations side of the business by formulating an E & P strategy, introducing improved oil recovery techniques in the existing fields on one hand and to intensifying exploration for new prospects in hitherto unexplored frontier areas on the other. The redevelopment project for the flagship Bombay High oilfield, initiated during this period in association with the reputed consultants, Gaffney Cline & Associates, is a case in point.

In addition to giving an added impetus to its core activities, Bora also diversified ONGC's energy resource base and ventured into non-conventional energy resources. He also expanded its business portfolio by initiating activities in related business areas such as coal bed methane that has today become an attractive proposition both for public and private sector companies.

Following his superannuation from ONGC in April 2001, Bora had been a much-in-demand technocrat, particularly in the petroleum and the related sectors. He had been a part-time independent director of GAIL, Gujarat Gas Company Ltd, Petronet LNG Ltd and Assam Hydrocarbon & Energy Company Ltd. Additionally, he had also been the non-executive chairman and independent director of Interlink Petroleum Ltd. He was also a trustee of the Lovraj Kumar Memorial Trust and member of Krishnamurthy Committee on Restructuring of Petroleum Sector Undertakings. He has also been and still is a part time adviser to a few consultancy and operating companies besides some entities of State governments and industry associations. He also had the distinction of being the President of the Assam Association, Delhi for two terms at a stretch.

Subir Raha Brought Transparency

(May 2001–May 2006)

*W*hen *Subir Raha joined ONGC on 25 May 2001,*
he had nursed no illusions about the intricacies
of the job, and the challenges that he would face. He
had brought to his new job 31 years of rich and varied
experience in the downstream sector in the Indian Oil
Corporation that included a stint as the Head of the
Oil Coordination Committee that was cockpit of sort
of the oil industry.

Though he was new to ONGC and the upstream sector, yet he was not a total stranger. Raha was, in fact, on the board of ONGC for seven months as a nominee of Indian Oil Corporation, after the two Hydrocarbon Navratna giants had swapped equity. He had wisely made use of that opportunity to take a couple of trips to the ONGC's offshore installations and got a good feel of the organization that he was to head seven months later.

He had also known that the country's most sought after position in the corporate public sector was not so cushy a

seat. Raha probably had an inkling of what he would be landing himself into. But the ground reality that he later found must have far exceeded the unease and the perception that he had had entertained of ONGC. On the very first day in office, he sent an open letter to about 40,000 of his colleagues greeting them as the CMD of this giant family. Raha had begun the letter by explaining his 31-year experience as a professional manager in the downstream hydrocarbon sector. Some of the recipients took the letter as an apologetic introduction since Raha did not have any experience in the upstream sector of the petroleum industry, forgetting that some of the most successful of ONGC's chairmen like KD Malaviya, LJ Johnson, NB Prasad and Col SP Wahi didn't have even a nodding acquaintance with petroleum as a subject. However, all of them had done their homework well enough to grasp its nitty-gritty.

Unmindful of the sceptics and doubting Thomases, Raha had gone ahead in expounding his philosophy and his expectations upfront in the very first letter. He wrote that the twin evils of corruption and complacence must be shunned and finally eliminated. He wanted each employee to measure his or her worth in terms of what he or she has created for ONGC.

Raha receiving degree in Electronics and Telecommunications Engineering at Jadavpur University

Raha's definition of integrity was somewhat unorthodox. Integrity, he had then explained was not merely shunning of bribes. 'Professional integrity' required that one performed a given job to the best of one's knowledge, experience, prudence, diligence and honesty.

Briefly, Raha had implored the large ONGC family in general, and its middle and senior cadres in particular to incorporate certain essential characteristics in their daily work culture. And these characteristics included competence, commitment and integrity. For Raha, integrity covered personal, professional and managerial attributes. Thus these three elements of integrity were the sine qua non of a true and dedicated manager. That was Raha's philosophy when he took over the reins of ONGC in May 2001.

One must assess some of Raha's achievements. Raha had greatly succeeded in introducing the concept of accountability in ONGC.No longer could the employees sit on files without someone asking questions. Complaints would be redressed promptly and explanations were sought. Disciplinary actions too were taken against those culpable. Norms for decision-making were fixed, and their violations taken note of. That concept was introduced at all levels of administration, and no one, however high, escaped the scrutiny.

Yet, there were instances where delinquent officers got away. The enforcement of rules and code of conduct in an organization as unwieldy as ONGC was not easy. And for accountability or any such concept to succeed, it must percolate right down the hierarchy. Mere propagation of a concept is not enough; it must also be diligently practiced.

That was a revolutionary step. Times were such that foreign vendors and suppliers were kept at arm's length. ONGC's officers were sternly told to avoid their company, though underhand deals continued to flourish. There was a director of stores and purchase who had sternly admonished his stores and purchase officer as his seven-year-old son used to play with my son; we were then next door neighbours, and my company, SK Oilfield Equipment Co. Pvt Ltd, was just seven years old. I later came to know that the director himself was among the most corrupt.

Raha's Major Achievement

Raha's major achievement was to bring about corporate democracy in its various manifestations. CMD's Open Forum, held during his visits to various assets and projects turned to be a big draw. Raha's speech would be typically in the format of an address by a chairman at the annual general meeting of a corporate.

Within six months, Raha had established two remarkable features. One, he made absolutely transparent the working of ONGC, and by extension his own thoughts, views, expressions and experiences. Two, he had set in motion an innovative system of accountability, hitherto conspicuously absent in the organization's work culture.

Introducing transparency in various facets of the functioning of ONGC was another achievement. Prior to Raha's arrival, everything was marked 'secret' or 'confidential'. Tender notices for purchases and specifications were most securely guarded, and their contents leaked only at a price. Raha put these on the ONGC's website; anyone could access these instantly and gratis.

Open sessions were conducted with vendors and suppliers in order to explain ONGC's procedures and policies in regard to purchases, and to seek their views and suggestions. The first was held in Mumbai a couple of years ago and the fifth one held as recently as 11 May. It would be revealing to quote a portion of Raha's speech at this Vendors' Meet.

'I will be setting up teams in each discipline to review thoroughly the specifications and you are most welcome to make your suggestions today, or before the end of May. It's known that the specifications need to be upgraded from time to time to keep pace with technology upgradation and best-in-the-class efficiency standards.'

Raha had raised several issues of mutual concern but those are beyond the pale of this piece. But it would suffice to state that this continuous interaction with vendors and contractors is one of the most transparent and sincere efforts initiated by Raha to win over the confidence of international and domestic vendors.

Transparency was his Signature Tune

Thus, transparency had become a hallmark in his proclaimed agenda of giving a new makeover to ONGC. Right from day one, Raha had correctly diagnosed ONGC's ailments. That ONGC had acquired, over the years, a shady, seedy and slovenly perception in the public mind was no secret at all. Raha had been aware of that image. But what perhaps even he had not realized, was the sweeping extent of the malaise that had corroded its very vitals. ONGC, despite many brilliant and dedicated professionals, who had, in their own way tried to keep aloft its flag, needed a major surgery in order to remove the all-pervasive complacency and lethargy. Thus, Raha quietly donned the white coat of a surgeon and carefully began the surgery.

He first tackled the utter lack of transparency that had given somewhat unnecessary and unwarranted powers to the *babus*. Decisions on purchases were kept closely guarded secrets. The case officer or his boss would invariably keep the connected file under lock and key so as to hide its contents even from his own colleagues. Not that the secrecy was intrinsically needed in the interest of ONGC, but it ensured that he alone was privy to the nitty-gritty of the tender to be able to barter away the secret information to the interested bidders.

That gave much scope for manipulation and *jalebi* making. Therefore, hardly any tender with the initial validity of 120 days, was ever decided within the stipulated period; not even tenders of proprietary nature. Technical comments too lost their sanctity and items were declared technically not acceptable (TNA) or technically acceptable (TA) at the whims of the indenter concerned, or whoever was given the task of technical evaluation of the bids.

Manipulation Rules the Roost

Worse, the L-1 (the lowest price) bidder would be made L-2 (second lowest price) by sheer sleight of pen by excluding or including the cost of spares. This practice continued for long and Raha also put all of that on the tenders' website. After all, what was the need of secrecy, since the public, or even limited tenders, were opened in the presence of the bidders.

Reverting to the concept of transparency introduced by Raha, one must admire his guts in putting on website every policy and major decision of ONGC which each one of its 40,000 employees could log in.

Open Letters—Hallmark of Raha's Tenure

More important and laudable has been the introduction of writing open letters in which he had described his own performance reports to the entire ONGC fraternity. The first of these open letters was sent on 25 May 2001, the day he took over as the CMD. In that letter, Raha had not only introduced himself, but had also penned his considered thoughts on the importance of competence, commitment and cohesion. He condemned the evils of complacence and corruption as well as defined these. History, he had written, taught them that empires were ruined whenever and wherever complacency crept in. Corruption, according to Raha, was not merely taking or giving of bribes. Corruption, he had added, also occurred in management when a decision was influenced by extraneous considerations. He also invited his colleagues in ONGC to write to him on his personal e-mail address, to share their thoughts on ONGC, and assured them of total confidentiality. Incidentally, Raha personally sent replies to individual mails. He worked till late in the night; I remember having received a mail from him sent at 1 a.m.

In this subsequent two letters dated 19 July and 14 August 2001, Raha had given details of the various policy decisions taken by ONGC. Just sample two of the sub-headings.

'Some of us wrote the Dream. All of us must make it happen.'

'We will give you the power. You must use it to benefit ONGC.'

The above sentences sum up Raha's philosophy and his agenda.

Raha's New Year letter in 2002 was not only the lengthiest but was also very touching. Let me quote him.

'As I write, 10% of my current tenure is over. Looking back over the first six months, and remembering the warm welcome that you kindly accorded me everywhere, the very first thing that comes to my mind is this: there is so much talent in our organization, so little of this capability is appreciated, and so much more that we can, we should, we must achieve. The next impressions are of wastage, corruption and delay, spoiling our technology, performance and image.'

He had cited three examples:

A woman petitioned that her unmarried son had died 10 years ago but the question of family pension had not been settled. A report was sought from the office concerned and promptly submitted. It put the entire blame on the hapless mother for (i) submitting late (after seven years) the request for the family pension and (ii) that the pension was only payable to the widow or the children and since the colleague had died unmarried, his mother was not entitled to the same. For those delinquent ONGC officers, one of the most disquieting qualities of Raha was his tenacity. He took to the rule book, and found a specific clause allowing family pension in the case of an unmarried employee.

The second was a petition from a small-time contractor whose bills were not being paid because of which he was thinking of committing self-immolation in utter desperation. Here too, the official report blamed the contractor. It said that the contractor was being paid, thereby implying that the complaint need not be pursued.

The third complaint pertained to a former colleague who wrote to Raha from abroad. It referred to *jalebi* making (my own expression) in an important tender, and the disgusted colleague decided to resign rather than fall in line and compromise on ethics. Raha found that the substance of the allegations was true.

Raha painfully shared three of the many such experiences he had encountered in the first six months. Here I again reproduce Raha's excellent prose:

> *'I have shared just three out of the many such experiences in these six months; I am sure that you have also felt the heartbreak, the anger, the frustration, many times. But did you ask why? Who violated the Value System? How do the same negligence, indifference, incompetence, greed and fraud happen time and again? The answer stares us in the face: all these things happen because some of us do it, many of us tolerate it, and the rest of us think it does not matter as long as our personal interests are not affected. It's the Enemy Within.'*

Raha's stewardship of ONGC has been impeccable. Now, ONGC is a serious global player rubbing shoulders with the major multinational oil giants and the top national oil companies in the corridors of the world energy sector. Raha has given ONGC a special makeover, something which every ONGCian should be proud of.

At the time of writing (23 May 2006), I was not aware if the government had given Raha a two-year extension which he richly and rightfully deserved. The matter of extending Raha's tenure was as much victim of the proverbial 11th hour syndrome as was his appointment five years before that.

Raha did not get any extension as was apprehended. He was too much of his own man, and the powers that be then wanted a henchman.

Radhey Shyam Sharma

(May 2006–January 2011)

*T*hough Radhey Shyam Sharma came from the profession of cost and works accountancy, he took to the oil industry as if he was born into it.

Since joining ONGC in July 1988 as Joint Director (Finance), Sharma made it a point to acquire experience in the wide and complex range of activities of this upstream industry. As its Director (Finance), he had made it a point to ask questions and go into numerous details involved in any project before it got his approval.

At the heart of all his initiatives was the need to change the value proposition, or value-for-cost-equation. His thrust on technology driven intensive exploration, restructuring of organizational system and multi-disciplinary team (MDT)

approach had paid rich dividends and yielded desired results. Sharma embraced a three-pronged strategy to sustain production levels: (a) expeditious development of discoveries, (b) arresting decline from the mature fields, and (c) augmenting production from overseas assets.

It was therefore no wonder that ONGC was able to produce 61.76 MTOE oil and gas in fiscal year 2008 which, so far, is the highest in its history.

ONGC Acquires New Global Brand Equity

The core instrument of ONGC's operation is the executive committee (EC) comprising of all functional directors and is chaired by CMD. This committee reviews ONGC's performance and other issues on a regular basis and takes necessary decisions and mid-course corrections, if required. Sharma strongly believed in collective leadership and consensus, but he nevertheless led the organization from the front. During his tenure (until 21 December 2010) the EC has held as many as 91 meetings covering 1,907 agenda items of which 130 related to the welfare of its workforce.

Under Sharma's leadership, ONGC has achieved new brand equity in the global E & P business. OVL (ONGC Videsh Ltd), its flagship, wholly owned subsidiary strides like a colossal on the international petroleum scene, and has become one of the most sought after partners in acquiring properties in third world countries.

At personal level, Sharma was the President of Global Compact Network, India (GCN) since May 2006, and provided a visionary leadership to the entire industry fraternity to encourage ethical business practices. He played a significant role in public sector (government) companies, and as a member of Standing Conferences of Public Enterprises (SCOPE) as well. Sharma has been proactive in promoting excellence. He was instrumental in winning ONGC many rewards, awards and accolades. He was essentially a simple man without any aura of arrogance or superiority, who was also very pro employee and believed that the employee is the most important stakeholder in an organization. He was equally interested in devising innovative schemes in order to help the retired workforce and had reportedly prepared an attractive financial package as a parting gift to the ex-ONGCians.

Ajit Kumar Hazarika

(February 2011–September 2011)

In December 2012, AK Hazarika was ONGC's senior most director holding the important charge of onshore operations.

He had earlier officiated for 9 months as its CMD, after RS Sharma had demitted his office on 1 February 2011. Hazarika's performance during his 9 months' tenure as the CMD was marked with much distinction.

Sudhir Vasudeva took charge from Hazarika on 3 October 2011 when he was appointed the permanent CMD.

Essentially a driller, Hazarika during his 35-year long association with ONGC was actively involved in its multifaceted activities. He specialized in cementing—an important and essential ingredient of drilling operations. His first assignment began in Assam and he remained there until 1989. In those 13 years, Hazarika held numerous important positions with increasing and complex responsibilities. It was to his credit that he discharged with dedication all the jobs given to him.

For all this meritorious work, Hazarika was declared, *Drilling Engineer of the Year 1990*.

Thereafter, Hazarika did not look back and achieved one success after another. In Chennai, he was given the important responsibility of heading an MDT to work on the prestigious Mumbai High redevelopment projects (north and south). His excellent contribution in drilling services was duly recognized, and Hazarika was elevated to the position of Head of Well Services in Mumbai in April 2002.

His next promotion came when he was made Executive Director and Chief–Well Services in January 2003 which confirmed his qualities of leadership and ability to manage people, both working with him and under him.

Hazarika reached the pinnacle of his profession when he was given the coveted job of director (onshore) in September 2004 by the Government of India. It was to his credit, that for seven years, he successfully fulfilled the wide and varied responsibilities spread across the country. He therefore became the longest serving ONGC Director.

There were seven onshore assets in India out of which six assets produced oil with associate gas. Only a single asset produced gas. ONGC had then been awarded 9 CBM blocks onshore, that were successfully completed. ONGC used state of the art technology by drilling horizontal wells passing through various coal seams with a view to procuring maximum quantity of gas from every well.

Hazarika was also a member of the Governing Council of Petroleum Federation of India (PETRO-FED) and was the Chairperson of SPE Delhi chapter in 2007.

Sudhir Vasudeva

(October 2011–February 2014)

*A*s CMD of ONGC, Sudhir Vasudeva was able to carve *a special niche for himself in the relatively short span of less than two years as its head honcho.*

His was not an easy job; two of his immediate predecessors RS Sharma and Subir Raha, had left a rich yet challenging legacy. It nevertheless goes to Vasudeva's credit that he took the challenging assignment in his long stride, and in no time, won the respect and admiration not only of the 33,000 ONGCians but also of his peers both in the public and private sectors.

With many of the discovered oil and gas fields in India's ageing and yielding declining production, OVL, ONGC's overseas arm, became the cornerstone of Vasudeva's special drive to boost India's oil and gas kitty by securing abroad more and more oil and gas properties. OVL then operated 33 projects in 15 countries, 10 of these properties are in the production stage and yielded 65 million boe during 2011–2012. By December 2012, OVL had made a cumulative investment amounting to $14 billion in its foreign assets and, with a war chest of $8.8 billion at its disposal, and was now poised for a quantum jump over the next five years. As a result, OVL now contributed 15% to India's oil and gas kitty.

A distinguished technocrat, Vasudeva was also the Chairman of OVL, having its corporate footprints in 15 countries across the globe. He also chaired the Board of Mangalore Refinery and Petrochemicals Ltd (MRPL) and five other ONGC Group companies. Needless to say, all the

Vasudeva was honoured with the Pride of Nation award by the Doon Citizens Council of which the author Raj Kanwar was then the president

companies in the ONGC Group were and continue to perform with much distinction.

Vasudeva was amongst the first generation engineers joining ONGC in the second batch of graduate engineers in 1976. He had brought to this coveted job, 34 years of rich experience in oil and gas activities in offshore waters, that also included 14 years in senior positions at the hierarchical and corporate levels.

Path-Breaking Initiatives

Credited with many path-breaking initiatives in the complex offshore project management, Vasudeva was also conferred with the coveted CEPM-PMA Fellowship on Project Management in 2011. Thoroughly groomed in the upstream petroleum business, he became the chairperson of Indian Council of Society of Petroleum Engineers (SPE) as well as the Director at-large in SPE International Board of Directors, a first by an Indian.

A chemical engineer (gold medalist) with an advanced diploma in management, Vasudeva believed in fostering active industry-academia relationship. He was the Chairperson of the Board of Governors of NIT, Raipur, a special invitee on the Board of Governors of Pandit Deendayal Petroleum University, Gujarat and a member on the board of Doon University.

ONGC today stands tall as India's most valuable *maharatna* public sector corporate and one of the most outstanding exploration and production companies in the world. Under Vasudeva's competent stewardship, ONGC achieved twin distinctions; it became the highest profit-making and highest dividend-paying corporate in the country. Additionally, ONGC was rated as one of the *Fortune's* Most Admired Companies in the world.

A visionary leader and a keen promoter of best practices in policy-making and enterprise management, Vasudeva had charted a Perspective Plan 2030 to carry forward the excellence of ONGC and to maintain its leadership position on the energy horizon of the country. No wonder then, that the Indian National Academy of Engineering in recognition of his meritorious contribution to the Engineering discipline at large conferred on Vasudeva its coveted fellowship (FNAE). The Institute of Chemical Engineers (IIChE), the apex body of chemical engineers, also felicitated him with a prestigious Honorary Fellowship.

Vasudeva became the first business leader from an Indian PSU to be a member of the board of the United Nation's Global Compact, the largest voluntary corporate citizenship initiative in the world, championing the cause of responsible business behaviour through its 10 principles in the areas of human rights, labour standards, the environment and anti-corruption. Additionally, he was also the President of Global Compact Network, India. For upholding the highest standard of corporate governance in the boards of ONGC Group of companies, he was presented with Distinguished Fellowship of Institute of Directors in August 2012.

CHAPTER 13

Shashi Shanker Takes ONGC to Heights of Excellence

When Shashi Shanker took over as the C&MD of ONGC on 1st October 2017, he had no illusions whatsoever about the gigantic task that faced him. For 36 long years, Shanker has been an inalienable part of India's energy colossus, and had seen its every nook and cranny. Thus in more ways than one, he is today one of the most experienced stalwarts of ONGC.

IT is his mission that ONGC must earnestly endeavour, as its vision stipulates, to become a global leader in the integrated energy business via sustainable growth, knowledge excellence and exemplary governing practices. As such, he is now seriously considering a new Vision Document, '*Strategic Roadmap 2040*' that would  not only propel its growth but would also ensure energy security for the Nation. The proposed document would recast the objectives of the ongoing '*Perspective Plan 2030*'.

Just 17 months into the job, Shanker has already established beyond any doubt his credentials as a go-getter and outstanding administrator. Organic growth via enhanced exploration in some of the more promising sedimentary basins has received his top priority. As a result, 12 oil and gas discoveries (six each offshore and onshore) were made in these basins in the very first fiscal, thereby raising the proved and probable reserves (2P) to 67.83 million metric tonnes of oil and oil equivalent gas (MMtoe). Significantly, one of these discoveries was made in a New Exploration & Licencing Policy (NELP) Block.

All this could be achieved, thanks to the extensive exploration carried out earlier both in the known and the Frontier basins. Significantly, two of these 12 discoveries, viz., *Mattur* West-1 (Cauvery onland) and *Matar* have already been monetized. *Mattur* West-1 started producing in May 2017 and *Matar* in January 2018.

Even the domestic crude oil production together with its share from profit sharing joint ventures rose by 2.5 per cent to 50.04 MMtoe during fiscal 2018 as compared to the output of 48.80 MMteo in the preceding year. Further, on standalone basis, oil production from ONGC's operated fields was 22.31 MMT during the fiscal 2017. Even this minimal increase in production is indicative of the efficient reservoir management and prudent technological interventions considering the fact that all these fields are of matured age. For the second consecutive year, natural gas production too showed a significant increase; it rose by six per cent to 23.48 Billion Cubic Meter (BCM) in fiscal 2018 as compared to 22.09 BCM in the preceding year.

Perspective Plan 2030 – Its Features

It was Sudhir Vasudeva who had taken a bold initiative in 2012 and launched an ambitious **Perspective Plan 2030**. It then aimed at achieving an output of 60 Mtoe and a six-fold growth by 2030 in production from its overseas operations. It had budgeted an investment of $176 billion that aimed at securing energy security for India as visualized by Prime Minister Narendra Modi. The then CMD DK Sarraf had felt that even though higher spending in a low oil price regime would have an adverse impact on ONGC's earnings, it didn't really have a choice.

However, Ajay Kumar Dwivedi, who had just then taken over as the exploration director at ONGC was quite optimistic. 'We will invest about 100 billion rupees during the current financial year and drill 50 wells including 10 shale wells.' Equally optimistic was ONGC offshore director TK Sengupta who too hoped that the days of stagnant production had ended and that ONGC would be able to sustain a steady rate of growth in future. It was then also planned to commence in fiscal 2019 the much delayed and highly anticipated production from Krishna-Godavari (KG) with a view to sustaining the rise in production. However, it was easier said than done. The ageing onshore fields had already reached the mode of *diminishing returns* and that could not be compensated by the marginal increase that came from offshore wells. Even four years after its launch, there was no noticeable movement or progress toward the targets set forth in the **Perspective Plan 2030**.

Strategic Roadmap 2040

It is thus a happy augury that Shashi Shanker is currently in the process of drawing up a **Strategic Roadmap 2040** that would reframe the vision, and recast the objectives of the **Perspective Plan 2030**, particularly in the context of the changed environment.

This achievement is all the more creditable considering that ONGC have had to contribute from time to time mind-boggling sums running into hundreds of thousand crore rupees by way of interim dividend to the kitty of government of India simply to help it meet its current account deficit.

In his Republic Day speech at Dehra Dun this year, Shanker had expressed his confidence that ONGC would reach greater heights of excellence that would uplift it to a whole new orbit of high performance. Lauding the contribution made by ONGCians, he voiced his firm belief that they were the best both in terms of competence as well as commitment to company's growth.

PART II

KDMIPE
A JEWEL IN ONGC'S CROWN

CHAPTER 14

The Infant Years

ONGC, if anything, invariably carried a streak of ambition. Its birth on 14 August 1956, was unheralded and received with a degree of cynicism by some sceptics in the government.

Despite the overzealous KD Malaviya being its biological father and Jawaharlal Nehru the foster father, ONGC was treated as a step-child by some of the ministers and the bureaucrats; it was denied proper upbringing and its childhood years passed from hand to mouth. Even a minor expense required an approval by the mandarins in New Delhi and at times its field survey parties could not receive their salaries due to late arrival of cheques or money orders.

Despite the nitpicking by bureaucrats, it continued on its chosen mission of finding oil in the country. And once oil was discovered in Cambay, and soon thereafter in Ankleshwar, things changed overnight. The bureaucrats became less sceptical, and slightly loosened the purse strings that they had held tightly until then.

Knowing very well that well-equipped laboratories are the very essence of an oil company, ONGC took urgent steps to set up its own laboratories. This difficult task was given by AMN Ghosh to SN Talukdar, a subaltern.

Earlier, Talukdar had been involved in imparting training to apprentice geologists and it was to its credit that he had meticulously performed that job. For a 27-year-old, those responsibilities, Talukdar later recalled, were challenging. With only a handful of staffers, he went about the job of setting up the organizational structure. First, he needed to find suitable premises, large enough to accommodate the laboratories. He zeroed in on the *Naaz* Building Complex, behind the old landmark, Kwality Restaurant. It took some time to acquire the elementary necessities—laboratory counters, tables, chairs, stools, few microscopes and other sundry items. The laboratories, Talukdar thought, must at least look like the well-equipped laboratory of a university.

Where to Find Talented Geoscientists?

The next problem was to find the requisite and qualified geoscientists to work as research guides and assistants. The stalwarts went scouting for suitable talent amongst the apprentice geoscientists from the 1956 batch; Malaviya, Ghosh and others used all of their persuasive skills to lure talent from universities and the multinationals. They were looking for people with aptitude in applied research, in basic life sciences like botany and zoology besides chemistry. All of those, who subsequently joined, had some inkling of the subjects. However, none had an idea of the role of those sciences in oil exploration. They were to work in three laboratories— chemistry, palynology and paleontology. Chemistry was fine; but the other two tongue-twisters were too new to be in the 1955 dictionary. In fact, the term 'palynology' had become part of the geoscientific lexicon only in 1943.

AK Ghosh was brought in from the Bose Research Institute, Calcutta to head the palynology laboratory. Next to follow was Dr CP Verma from Lucknow's Birbal Sahni Institute. The next round of fast-paced recruitment took a different course. Freshers with rudimentary experience in laboratory work responded to newspaper advertisements. YK Mathur and Annie Thomas joined the ranks.

Ruby Kumar with Raj Kapoor and wife Krishna in Moscow in July 1965

The chemists were more confident and wore their knowledge on their shirt-sleeves. MM Dey had initially joined as a field chemist in Jwalamukhi, and had had a brush with Tagiev, the Russian drilling consultant. The story of his getting the better of Tagiev had become common knowledge in ONGC, and that had given Dey a special aura. Such was the confidence of some of the chemists those days. They carried the same confidence into the corridors of the chemistry laboratory where Dey would keep the lab crowd spellbound with his exploits in the 1940s. In the absence of a centrifuge, the chemists in the earlier days would tie up the test tube with mud to a fan; sometimes, the tube broke and the ceiling and walls bore the brunt of the scattering mud.

'Among the awe-struck scientists was Ruby G Singh (she later married Krishan Kumar of 1956 batch of young pioneers) who had joined ONGC just about then, after obtaining her master's degree in chemistry. She voluntarily retired in early 1990s as Deputy General Manager on the superannuation of her husband. She was the top woman scientist in the geochemistry division at KDMIPE.' Dr PR Sinha became a source of inspiration for generations of chemists. SN Bhattacharya, Dr Indra and others gave that vital push into understanding the intricacies of drilling mud.

More Soviet Experts Arrive

All of them, with basic scientific knowledge, awaited the arrival of the Soviet expert, Dr Natalay Dmitrievna Mtchedlishvili, from VINGRI (Oil Institute) in Leningrad. She had left her family behind in Leningrad just to be able to introduce the Indian scientists to the world of palynology in oil exploration. Natalay came with five others to teach the basics to that team of neo-scientists. In the absence of computers in those early days of May 1957, her hand-prepared atlases of pollens and spores proved invaluable.

Ms Nina Nikolaevna Subbotina and Ms Paula Severyanovna Lubimova took charge of the micro palaeontology laboratory. Prof. VB Tatarsky and Victor K Vassilenko took over the reins of the sedimentary petrology division. They introduced an unconventional culture in laboratory work; there were no fixed working hours. If there was a job at hand, it had to be done without looking at the clock. The Russians were a hard-working lot; their attitude had a cascading effect on everyone.

The Geophysical Laboratory

The geophysical laboratories were set up in the rented *Santiniketan* Building at 103 Rajpur Road. With his GSI background, MA Ganapathy was made in-charge. He was given the unenviable task of organizing the logistics for the field parties, equipment and repairs. Krishan Kumar, Thirumalai, Shukla and Joseph Koithare from the batch of 1956, were also taken on board. The laboratories housed the machine shop, the seismic and electro-logging sections. A vehicle repair shop, surprisingly, was also added. Ganapathy and his team spent days and nights poring over electronics books, manuals and any available source material to understand the specifications of a variety of equipment and instruments. Everything had to be organized from scratch—explosives, detonators and miles of electrical wires, geophones, vehicles, repair kits and vital instruments. And, then, the logistics of dispatching the equipment to far-flung areas of the country was another ponderous job. In the off-season, from August to October, all the instruments would be brought to Dehra Dun for routine maintenance, and repairs. They needed mechanics. As luck would have it, the Commission could get some of the most gifted mechanics in its ranks. Usman Khan, a strapping Pathan from Afghanistan joined as a mechanic. He could repair anything mechanical.

Multi-Talented GD Sharma

Another person, GD Sharma, who joined, would ultimately leave his footprints in every oil province. Whether it was a simple vehicle or machine repair or book binding or shothole rig or electronics repair, GD could fix anything and everything. He had had a colourful career and eventually retired as a general manager in drilling. He was also instrumental in introducing the concept of contract drilling by cooperatives of retired ONGCians. He lives an active life today, at his spacious Idgah residence in Dehra Dun.

There was a wealth of information coming from the virgin sedimentary basins of the country that needed to be examined and coordinated. Negi was the boss, and a hard task master too. During the off-season, Negi, Hari Narain, SN Sengupta, AM Awasthi and other seniors would keep a hawk-like eye on the quality of maps and reports prepared.

The paleontology laboratory was headed by SN Singh, a professor from Lucknow University. AK Datta, a geologist working in the fields of *Jwalamukhi*, was recalled to Dehra Dun. His postgraduate thesis was on micro-palaeontology. DK Guha and BN Srivastava also joined the ranks.

PV Dehadrai took over the reins of the Petrology laboratory. He was soon joined by a dynamo in the person of Dr ATR Raju, an indefatigable field geologist. Dr V Raghavendra Rao, with a stint as an Assistant Professor in Mysore University and in GSI, had specialized in microscopic fossils at the University of Adelaide; he was another natural choice.

MC Poddar, with his rich experience in GSI, became the head of the geological laboratories. The painstaking process of procurement of microscopes and slides began. As MBR Rao had put it, the Commission did not hesitate in spending money for essential instruments. The laboratories got the best of instruments available in the world. Austerity on personal comforts, however, was an unwritten code in every sphere of activity. The bare interiors of the laboratory with wooden partitions became home to the extended family of Russians and their Indian understudies. In winters, small charcoal-fired *anghitis* kept them warm.

One winter night, at seven, AMN Ghosh was driving past the Naaz Building. On seeing the lights on, he stopped and peered inside; YK Mathur was working on some models for an industrial exhibition. He entered, and requested Mathur

PROF. N.A.EREMENKO

SANTOSH.

ON YOUR 50th BIRTHDAY WE GREET YOU

(V.V. SASTRI)
(S.N. BHATTACHARYA)
(INDERJIT SINGH)
(D.N. AVASTHI)
(V.K. ARORA)
(V.K. VERMA)
(A.T.R. RAJU)

D. DUN
22nd. June, 68.

to prepare one extra model of spores with plaster of paris. Watching intently for a long hour, he got up and gave a pat on Mathur's back. That was to be his greatest reward in life—a compliment from Ghosh to a junior technician.

Dr G Erdtman, an eminent palynologist from Sweden, visited the laboratories, and had had a lively interaction with the team of Russians and Indians. The German experts, Profs Schott and Richter came calling in 1957. Malaviya too visited the laboratories along with Mahavir Tyagi, Deputy Minister for Defence and a popular Dehra Dun MP; he inaugurated the ONGC Recreation Club of which PN Rajaram of the class of 1956 became the first president. The scientists and others would play table tennis during the lunch break and after office hours; additionally, there was a carom table for carom enthusiasts.

A library section came up in Naaz Building. Every week, AMN Ghosh would check the new arrivals and ask Ganguly to get important chapters cyclostyled. Later, they were distributed among the scientific community. The books reflected the immediate need of the hour. Some of the earliest collections included titles like 'Sheet Metal Shop Practices', 'Fundamentals of Carpentry', 'Electronics', 'Physical Chemistry of The Hydrocarbons', 'The Science of Petroleum', 'This Fascinating Oil Business', and many others. A newsletter also started appearing on the shelves. This ONGC newsletter would be a one-stop window for all ongoing activities. Employees were encouraged to write articles on their respective areas of specialization.

CHAPTER 15

Research and Training:
The Adolescent Years

The Naaz Building laboratories were to prove very handy; under the guidance of stalwarts such like AMN Ghosh, Dr Hari Narain, SN Sengupta, AM Awasthi and others, it more than justified its raison d'être. Yet, it did not truly reflect the fond beliefs of ONGC's founding fathers who had always dreamt of having a top of the class research and training institute. By its very nature and physical constraints, the Naaz Building was, at best, a stop-gap arrangement.

Scores of ONGC's geoscientists, engineers and drillers had gone abroad since 1959 and were trained in some of the best research laboratories and drill sites. Even KD Malaviya himself had visited many of these world-class laboratories and desperately yearned to replicate those top-of-the-class laboratories in India. But what deterred him was the shortage of funds and absence of requisite expertise.

The world had long moved away from seepages and hit and run discoveries to basin modelling and geochemical research to identify the reservoirs better. The chronology of oil research enunciated the growth of research in the oil industry—cut and try (before 1915), measurement and correlation (1915–1935) and analysis and synthesis (1936–1965). And by 1965, it had, with the advent of computers, moved up a step to systematization. ONGC needed to catch up on that technology in the shortest possible time. The Naaz Building was just about a modest start.

A small group was set up. It conducted a study of the state of scientific research in the oil industry and the expenses involved. By that time, the major oil companies were found to be spending up to 2 per cent of their budget for research projects. They also employed about 3 per cent of their manpower in research and development.

A Separate Research Entity

Thus was born the need to set up a separate research entity with manpower drawn from various directorates. In order to attract the right talent, a 15 per cent research allowance was included in the proposal as a counterpoise to the project allowance that was then being given to the field personnel. It also envisaged the direct recruitment of scientists.

ONGC then submitted the study report to the Planning Commission for budgetary approval under the Third Five-Year Plan (1961–1965). The Planning Commission, in its wisdom, approved a total allocation of ₹180 crores for the Commission as a whole. It was a major victory for Malaviya, who had almost gone down on his knees for ₹300 million five years earlier. The refreshing change in the bureaucratic mindset came because of the discovery of oil in Gujarat. The Planning Commission had also approved ₹25 million for research and training. An additional ₹100 million was approved for offices, colonies and laboratories.

A Knight Rider

A knight rider then came on a white charger in the shape of United Nations Development Programme (UNDP). Its finance arm, United National Special Fund (UNSF) granted an amount of $8,00,000 with the stipulation that the Indian government would come up with a matching commitment of 60 lakhs. There was, however, a caveat; UNDP was to appoint its own project manager. Several names of American and other western scientists were on the panel of UNDP but Malaviya preferred some reputed Russian scientist since most of the overseas experts at that time in ONGC were Russians, and Malaviya rightly felt that a Russian expat as a project manager of the research institute would be more effective. The choice eventually fell on Prof. NA Eremenko, an eminent petroleum geologist and geochemist from the All Union Institute of Petroleum Geology, Moscow. The Government of India on 12 June 1962 signed an agreement with the UNDP. The agreement also had a Plan of Operation (PoP) that was to serve as a guideline of sorts. Thus was conceived the Research & Training Institute (R&TI). Dr Hari Narain had earlier been appointed as its first director on 1 March 1962.

Prof. Eremenko joined in December the same year.

The main objective of the institute was to act as a nodal agency for applied research into all aspects of oil exploration and development. Its first task was to undertake basin studies of various sedimentary basins in India and to submit recommendations regarding regional oil prospects. The second objective was to submit to the Commission, independent second opinion based on reinterpretation and reassessment of scientific and technical data regarding exploration.

A private building was rented at 9 Cross Road, Dehra Dun. With four large rooms, two side rooms and two glazed verandahs, the accommodation seemed just enough. The PoP had stipulated employment of 72 staffers of which 36 were to be of technical background while the remaining were from general categories such as administration, finance, stores and so on.

Virender Kumar Verma and Kundan Lal Goyal were amongst the first technical personnel to have joined this infant institute while Krishan Veer provided the administrative support. VLN Sastry, Dr VR Rao, Dr SN Bhattacharya, DN Awasthi and S Srinivasan joined during the following few months as assistant directors responsible for their respective disciplines. Dr Amlendu Ray joined as Deputy Director. Additionally, in the course of time, eight senior scientific officers, 12 scientific officers and two senior technical assistants came on the roll of the institute.

The Russians Arrive

A large number of Russian scientists too came to give the nascent institute an international flavour. Among the first Russian experts were Sherkovesky (Reservoir), Mamdevo (Production), Belov (Drilling), Kasyanov (Geology) and Itenburg (Logging). Later, two expat geophysicists, Nomokonov and Molosin also joined their compatriots. With all these Russian specialists, an interpreter was an essential baggage who came in the person of one Pashkov. An Indian lady Ms Minhas was also employed as a Russian interpreter.

Divided into five divisions—geology, geophysics, geochemistry, drilling and training and economics, the institute seriously started working on its mandate. Hari Narain was essentially a research scientist and brought to bear on his new job all the experience that he had gained in Australia. Though strict and firm, he was nevertheless soft-hearted. The atmosphere at the institute was somewhat relaxed and a mutual bonhomie of sorts developed among the staffers who were until then mostly strangers.

'Things were unbelievably inexpensive those days', says KL Goyal who would go to Delhi with some colleagues with just ₹5,000 as advance to purchase laboratory equipment and chemicals. 'We could buy our entire requirement on the spot with this cash given to us,' he now recalls. A used *Honeywell 400 computer* was given gratis to ONGC by the US Government together with spares for five years' operations. KN Bhave at that time headed the computerization drive. 'None of us then knew anything about computers; we were sent to IIT Kanpur for a special crash course in computers,' adds Goyal. Thus scores of scientists were trained to operate the new computer; it was a tape-driven unit with a relatively good and fast printer. With this computer, collection and collation of data underwent a revolutionary change. The grant of $800,000 was intended both to import crucial equipment and to pay the salaries of the project manager and other overseas specialists. The first consignment of the imported equipment was worth $14,000 and that included a GE X-Ray Diffractometer and a RUSKA PVT while the Indian equipment cost just about ₹60,000. A dollar at that time was equivalent to ₹4.75.

And Now the Training

Training was a different ball game altogether; the limited space at 9 Cross Road was not enough to accommodate even the existing research staff.

In the meantime, the geology directorate had rented a large old bungalow at 40 East Canal Road; it generously allowed R&TI to make use of its verandahs for conducting its training classes. Thus the training division of R&TI made a humble beginning in a verandah; ONGCians had by then learnt to lead a life of austerity and deprivation. Later, ONGC rented a larger house, Padmini Niwas, on Raipur Road for the training centre.

It would be relevant here to underscore the sterling contribution made by the earlier pioneers in giving a definite shape and direction to research and development activities at the institute. The foremost was Founder Director Dr Hari Narain whose contribution to the growth of research and development segment of the Indian oil industry was phenomenal. In fact, the entire R&D project was essentially visualized and put in place by him. It was just unfortunate that he left ONGC in 1964 to join as Director of the newly formed National Geophysical Research Institute in Hyderabad. Dr Deb Kumar Chandra as Director in-Charge briefly replaced him before he was transferred to Assam as the Chief Geologist.

Gautam Kohli was the next director and he impressed one and all with his sincerity and integrity. It was a pity that Gautam died in a tragic air crash over Mont Blanc on 24 January 1966. India's leading nuclear scientist Dr Homi J Bhabha too, was a fellow passenger on that ill-fated flight.

The operations at R&TI were going apace and it was increasingly being realized that a new and much larger building would be needed if the research and training sections of the ONGC business were to be put on a larger canvas. The Kaulagarh Tea Estate was almost at the rear of Tel Bhawan and it was considered prudent to purchase the same for housing the R&TI. The expansive tea estate was large enough to accommodate the ONGC residential complex.

Now to Kaulagarh Road

LP Mathur was the next director and the first one to occupy the brand new office at 9 Kaulagarh Road. VV Sastri was the additional director and elevated in 1967 as its head on Mathur's retirement. Sastri was an inspirational leader and continued to hold fort until 1972 when R&TI assumed its new avatar as Institute of Petroleum Exploration (IPE). This change in the nomenclature of R&TI to IPE came about following the restructuring of ONGC by NB Prasad. Thus, in this reshuffle, SN Talukdar became the Director of the rechristened IPE. In his wisdom, Prasad also simultaneously merged the directorates of geology and geophysics into IPE.

Some other lasting contributions by R&TI were the setting up of a library, map and drawing section and a museum; it also published a scientific bulletin and its first issue appeared in 1962. The museum was, in fact, a part of the agreement signed between the UNDP and the Government of India. Here, one must mention the outstanding contribution of a young geologist Suresh Kumar in setting up the museum that vividly showcased the entire spectrum of ONGC's E&P activities. Much later on 19 December 2005, the museum was renamed Kalinin Museum during the tenure of Dr D Ray. The renamed and enlarged museum was formally inaugurated by Subir Raha.

CHAPTER 16

Research and Development:
The Adult Years

A s its activities and scope expanded, it was given the new name of the Institute of Petroleum Exploration (IPE) in 1971. Again, 10 years later, on 19 December 1981, the Institute of Petroleum (IPE) was renamed Keshava Deva Malaviya Institute of Petroleum Exploration (KDMIPE) to commemorate the memory of KD Malaviya, considered to be Father of the Indian Oil Industry.

It was red letter day for the geoscientists and the engineers who had worked hard and steadfastly during the past two decades. Prime Minister Indira Gandhi specially came to preside over the renaming function. This was also intended to be her personal tribute to Keshava Deva Malaviya who had been a longtime confidant and trusted lieutenant of her father, Jawaharlal Nehru. In fact, this research, development and training institute was as much due to the persistent and untiring efforts of Malaviya as the Oil & Natural Gas Commission was. The only difference was that the birth of the ONGC had gone through severe labour pains while the research and development set up had had a normal birth.

Indira Gandhi Renames IPE

IT was an impressive function and Indira Gandhi was very generous and effusive in her praise for KD Malaviya.

Professor NA Eremenko greeting Prime Minister Indira Gandhi in a traditional Russian style

'Memories of Shri Malaviya's dynamism and his dedicated persistence in the face of tremendous odds are fresh in my mind. Until the very end, he remained steadfast in developing and properly utilizing our national oil resources. This is an occasion to reflect on the larger aspects of the question that motivated our indigenous effort when the going was really tough and the scene was dominated by multinational oil companies. The ONGC was a David in the company of Goliaths. However, after the maiden discovery of oil in Gujarat in 1958, the progress to Bombay High via Assam has been smooth and sometimes spectacular.

These developments have, no doubt, benefited our economy, yet we have not gone far enough. Oil imported at high cost is still a major drain on our resources.'

– Indira Gandhi

She had then urged ONGC to further step up its efforts in oil exploration and exploitation with the same spirit of enthusiasm and dedication with which the organization had functioned since its inception. In the same context, she referred to the role of research and development and added that:

'ONGC will have to make an even bigger effort at oil exploration and exploitation. Research and development are important aspects of all such endeavours, especially because our goal of self-reliance is still far away. This Institute is significant for our R&D effort. It is our premier Geo-scientific Institute to explore Hydrocarbons. Since 1962, it has undertaken basin studies, evaluated geo-thermal prospects, developed new techniques for stimulation of well studies, effluent disposal and toxicity. It has also conducted a number of training courses both for Indians and foreigners. I am glad that the Institute of Petroleum Exploration has obtained a contract for research study in Abu Dhabi. It is apt that the Institute is named after Shri KD Malaviya at a time when it is poised for much bigger research and development. I expect this to be linked directly to the further steps for the onshore and offshore exploration and exploitation. More and more data from the wells will need to be evaluated by computers for which, I believe, the Institute is fully equipped.'

Sitting on the podium at that time were KD Malaviya's family including his wife Durga Malaviya, son Devendra

Asha Sheth–Malaviya's daughter
Courtesy: Naresh Patel

Malaviya and daughter Asha Sheth. The praise that Indira Gandhi had showered on Malaviya had touched some tender chord in Mrs Malaviya's heart and those present at the function saw tears in her eyes. Devendra and Asha too were very touched by the tribute paid to their father by India's Prime Minister. The renaming function was attended among others by the Minister of Petroleum PC Sethi, Uttar Pradesh Chief Minister VP Singh besides of course ONGC Chairman Col SP Wahi and member exploration, SN Talukdar.

A Nodal Agency

Returning to the narrative, it needs to be mentioned that, in a nutshell, KDMIPE is operating as the nodal agency for multidisciplinary synergistic basin scale and domain specific research in exploration. In 2012, it had over 300 highly experienced scientists in the domain of geoscientific research, E & P data management and resource and acreage appraisal of overseas properties that are sought to be acquired by OVL. Some of its main achievements are enumerated below:

- The most significant was the preparation of the first ever tectonic map of India in 1968 with the help of Russian specialists. In the 1960s, plate tectonics as a research subject was barely a decade old. It actually postulated that the earth consisted of huge plates which constantly moved relative to each other. Those plates, hundreds of kilometers thick, played a decisive role in our understanding of the migration and accumulation of oil and other minerals. It was a major breakthrough. As a famous geologist had said, '...even if we do not believe in flying saucers, we cannot ignore floating plates'.
- The final output had the signatures of the stalwarts from both the sides. BS Negi, BS Deshpande, SN Talukdar, VV Sastri, ATR Raju and AK Datta represented ONGC while the Russians were led by Eremenko, MV Kasianov, AM Seregin, IP Sokolov and AI Pavlenkov.
- After 36 years, in 2003, a new tectonic map of India was brought out. For this achievement, KDMIPE was awarded the National Mineral Award.
- KDMIPE had started processing digital data way back in 1971 with the introduction of a dedicated computer system, TIOPS-880. This computer had 24K word memory, which could process analog as well as digital data. With the CDP technique in use, and the huge amount of data acquired at offshore, the need to process a much larger volume of data was direly felt. Thus, the introduction of IBM-370/145 computer with

MVS operating system which had 1 MB memory and an array processor, in 1975, was a quantum jump in the seismic data processing. It greatly helped to meet the processing needs of both the onshore and offshore 2D data acquired by ONGC. This computer was equipped with PHOENIX application software. Data was processed by creating punch cards for individual jobs.

- An important idea that the institute conceptualized pertained to the regional mapping of Gulf of Cambay with the help of a Russian seismic vessel, *Academic Arkhangelsky*. Its outcome was fortuitous and resulted in the discovery of a structure in the offshore area that was then called Bombay High that turned out to be one of the most prolific fields. Later in 1973, ONGC acquired *Sagar Samrat* and drilled in that area. The rest is history.

- During the late 1970s and early 1980s, KDMIPE was instrumental in taking up science and technology (S&T) projects. Under the National Council for Science and Technology, S&T projects were formulated at KDMIPE which helped import or transfer high-tech instruments and technologies. Those were instrumental in developing various geochemical techniques and models with reference to the origin, migration and occurrence of each sedimentary basin.

- Prior to the 1980s, KDMIPE was the only agency and the research and development (R&D) nerve centre which regulated the corporate goals and formulated exploration strategies to achieve them within India and abroad.

- A detailed morphotectonic analysis on LANDSAT imageries in order to map the inaccessible areas was carried out. This led to the discovery of hidden structure in Cachar and Tripura.

- Another first of its kind work done by KDMIPE related

to the resource appraisal of Category I to Category IV sedimentary basins of India.

- Yet another significant contribution by KDMIPE has been the detailed evaluation of foreign acreage that it did and made suitable recommendations for farm-in opportunities for international cooperation and collaboration.
- KDMIPE also made the first ever geological map of the tertiary belt of the Himalayan foothills.
- The institute has mapped several prospects with techno-economic viability in different basins that has led to many important discoveries over the years.
- KDMIPE geoscientists compiled the first ever basic gravity map of India which helped in visualizing the variations in the sedimentary basins at sub-crustal levels.
- The institute conceptualized ISRAG (Indo-Soviet Research and Advisory Group) in 1990 for carrying out the resource assessment of sedimentary basins of India, which has been a benchmark achievement.
- KDMIPE prepared the sedimentary basin map of India—a tectonic classification (1987–1991). It conceptualized the Indo-British collaboration project with British Petroleum on the prospective analysis of the Himalayas.
- KDMIPE has also been instrumental in organizing first time national seminars on 'Petroliferous Basins of India' which deliberated on the latest dimension and technical issues of numerous sedimentary basins in the country. The last of such seminars were held in 1982 and 1992.
- KDMIPE took the lead in the preparation of litho stratigraphic documents of Indian petroliferous basins, which was the first detailed appraisal of the different sedimentary basins of India from the perspective of petroleum geology.
- With a view to sharing knowledge and state of

the art technologies at an international level, the institute organized international conferences such as PETROTECH (first conference in 1995) and International Conference on Petroleum Geochemistry and Exploration in the Afro-Asian Region (in 1985 and 2000). Now these conferences have been institutionalized at national and international levels, and are regularly being held.

- KDMIPE also conceptualized the idea of OIIS (ONGC Institutes Integrated Services) now known as COIN (Coordination of ONGC Institutes) to maximize opportunities of keeping the R & D infrastructure productive by way of revenue generating services.
- The Institute introduced the appraisal of gas hydrate prospects and prioritized KG Offshore for ONGC's first joint venture with United States Geological Survey (USGS), ARC and NRL, USA. It also helped in the preparation of a gas-hydrate anomaly map of India.
- It took initiative for greater coordination with the Oil Industry Development Board (OIDB) and firmed up guidelines for OIDB funding for various exploration projects.
- KDMIPE has implemented sequence stratigraphic studies of all the basins under the direction of the director (exploration).
- The institute has been playing a very significant and vital role in providing acreage evaluation for ONGC to the Director General of Hydrocarbons when the NELP and PEL regimes began. KDMIPE has also entered into collaboration with numerous national and foreign universities and institutes. Its Indian partners are CSIR/DST institutes like National Institute of Oceanography, Goa, National Geophysical Research Institute, Hyderabad, Wadia Institute of Himalayan Geology (WIHG), Dehra Dun etc. Other

such institutes include Andhra University, Benaras Hindu University and Calcutta University besides the Indian Institutes of Technology at Kharagpur and Kanpur, Indian School of Mines, Dhanbad and Dibrugarh University. Its international research partners are ARC (USA), Canada, UNOCAL Oregon State University, EGI (USA), BGRG (Germany), French Institute of Petroleum (IFP), University of Southern California, Cambridge University and Petroleum Gas University of Ploiesti, Romania.

- The institute was also instrumental in starting Project *Saraswati*. The project is aimed at finding deep aquifers in Rajasthan and other parts of the country. It also includes identification of deeper aquifers not yet exploited by other agencies. Accordingly, a study has been initiated in western Rajasthan covering 13 districts under a Memorandum of Understanding (MoU) with Water and Power Consultancy Service Ltd (WAPCOS), India, a government consultant, to identify and delineate broad areas for deep ground water exploration.

- On the industry-academia front, the institute has been providing summer trainings, dissertation support and internships to students in various exploration sciences over the years, to give them greater exposure so as to enhance their ability and qualifications for suitable openings in the industry.

- Incidentally, KDMIPE's more important achievements have been in the non-conventional hydrocarbons such as gas hydrate, shale gas, coal bed methane etc. It has given a big impetus to these non-conventional products and thus helped ONGC enter these new areas.

- KDMIPE is the nodal agency of Shale Gas Exploration-related R&D of ONGC. The Commission created a landmark in the exploration history of India for unconventional hydrocarbons, when gas flowed out on 25 January 2011 from the Barren Measure shale at a depth of around 1,700 meters in its first R & D well, RNSG-1, near Durgapur at Icchapur, West Bengal. That breakthrough was significant as India was the first Asian country, outside of USA and Canada where gas was discovered from shale. This breakthrough has been made possible due to systematic studies being made at KDMIPE in many of the shale formations in the various sedimentary basins. The initial studies indicate promising prospects in Damodar, Cambay, Krishna, Godavari and Kaveri basins. The potential of these basins has also been vetted by international experts.

Gas Hydrate

ONGC has been actively engaged through its Gas Hydrate division in the field of gas hydrate exploration since 1997. About 1,400 square kilometers area in the Krishna-Godavari offshore was identified for gas hydrate studies and 15 locations were pinpointed for drilling and coring operations under the aegis of First National Gas Hydrate Program (NGHP-1). Three prospective areas in the Krishna-Godavari Basin comprising 1,800 square kilometers (approx.) had been identified for the NGHP-02 expedition envisaged during 2011.

Basement Exploration

KDMIPE has been developing methodology for oil exploration in fractured basement and has assessed the hydrocarbon potential of Bombay High and Heera fields (Western Offshore Basin), Kumbakonam Horst (Kaveri Basin) and the Padra-Karjan area (Cambay Basin). Prospective areas for basement exploration are identified with state of the art interpretation software for fracture identification.

Coal Bed Methane

Coal Bed Methane (CBM) exploration was initiated as a joint R & D endeavour by KDMIPE and ONGC in 1995 in the Durgapur depression of the Raniganj Basin. Two R & D wells, DU-1 (DUAA) and DU-2 (DUAB), were drilled for evaluating the CBM potential of the area. Subsequently, ONGC carried out an evaluation of India's coalfields in 1997 and prioritized the coal basins of India as potential targets for CBM exploration. This foresight of the company yielded fruit when the company's first R & D well in the Jharia coalfield flowed methane in September 1997.

Greatly encouraged by this success, three more R & D CBM wells were drilled in the Parbatpur sector of the Jharia coalfield. Well JH#2 was kept under prolonged production testing and a sustained flow of methane at 6,000 m3/d from five objects (commingled) was established. In 2012, ONGC had five CBM acreages.

CHAPTER 17

Men Behind KDMIPE

*K*DMIPE *in its three avatars has had the good fortune of having some of the most dedicated scientists who sat at the top rung of its ladder. It was just fortuitous that its first director, Dr Hari Narain—a versatile research scientist—enjoyed an enviable reputation, and that its current head (2012) PK Bhowmick too should be an eminent and innovative geologist.*

During the past 50 years, there have been 19 directors, most of them bearing excellent credentials. They were men of varying nature and temperament, yet in their own ways they tried to perform their duties as they thought fit. Here in this chapter are profiled the brief stories of some of these men of destiny.

ONGC's director (exploration) is the administrative head of KDMIPE. The first of these members (or directors) was the redoubtable AMN Ghosh who, in fact, was also the first director of ONGC. The AMN Ghosh Auditorium at KDMIPE is a monumental reminder of the great contribution made by Ghosh. Other important members or directors were the other stalwarts, MBR Rao, LP Mathur and BS Negi.

There have been 12 directors who were designated members before ONGC became a corporate entity. It would only be appropriate to have their career graphs profiled in the pages of this history.

Dr Hari Narain

(March 1962–February 1964)

I wonder if a chairman of Johnson's stature would write so beseechingly to someone, irrespective of his status, credentials and other qualifications. His was certainly an unusual letter. What explains Dr Hari Narain's hesitancy could be the reluctance of National Geophysical Research Institute (NGRI) to release him. Dr Narain was also in touch with Indira Gandhi who was the Chairman of CSIR of which NGRI was a constituent entity.

The credit for conceptualizing the nucleus of a research institute in upstream petroleum sector would rightly go to Dr Hari Narain who was given this onerous task of preparing its blueprint by KD Malaviya. He was the Founder Director of the RTI; it was the name given to KDMIPE at its birth in 1962. Even after he had become  Director of NGRI, Hyderabad in 1964, Dr Narain continued to take interest in steering in the right direction the growth of research and development activities in ONGC.

Why a Research Institute?

In a note specially submitted in mid 1960s on the reorganization of ONGC to the Review Committee, Dr Narain had again stressed on the need for setting up an RTI in order to 'provide the scientific and technical leadership, and independent assessment of field data for both short-term and long-term planning'.

It should also find solutions to field, laboratory and theoretical problems encountered in the operations of the Commission. Further, it must keep the Commission informed of the developments in the industry and the latest operational techniques.

It must also provide training to all categories of staff to do their job more effectively. To achieve the above objectives, it should be manned by best scientists and engineers of the Commission. There should be provision of inter-transfer of scientists and a staff among the various component units of the Commission, to meet the requirements of the institute.

Training at all levels is an essential part of any scientific and technological endeavour. Intensive courses for new recruits and periodical refresher courses should be organized for all categories and age groups.

His Report was given due respect by the members of the Review Committee and included in its recommendations.

Dr Hari Narain, who was born in 1922, died on 27 January 2012; it is a pity indeed that he did not live a little longer to see the Golden Jubilee glory of the institute he had helped set up in 1962 and then nurtured.

That ONGC recognized all of his efforts was evident from the fact that five years after he had joined NGRI, ONGC still wanted him back as Director of Research and Training Institute. In a

letter dated 3 July 1969, Brig SC Vyas, Director of Administration, formally offered Dr Narain the post of the Director at RTI. The Commission also decided to offer him the maximum pay of ₹2,250 in the scale of 2,000-125-2,250. It meant that Dr Narain was being given 18 advance increments. As per the existing norms then, only five advance increments were permissible as a special case. Additionally, the Commission also offered him a Research Allowance at 15 per cent of the basic pay which was ₹337.50 and travel expenses for him and his family from Hyderabad to Dehra Dun.

The Reluctant Dr Hari Narain

Dr Hari Narain, it would appear, was not so keen to return to ONGC and possibly kept quiet on this tempting offer. Leslie J Johnson, ONGC's Chairman at that time, sent a personal letter on 3 December 1969, urging him to let him know when he would join RTI as its director. It is interesting to reproduce here what Johnson wrote.

'We have not yet heard from you if you accept the post of Director (Institute of Petroleum Exploration), at Dehra Dun, and, if so, when you expect to join. When you last met me, you had said that you were very likely to join sometime in early November. We have now come into December, and have not yet heard from you. In anticipation of your joining us fairly soon, I have held up recruitment to vacant posts at the Institute, and have also deferred promotions.

Staffers are now getting very restive, and it is not possible for me to put off these matters much longer. For this reason, I would be grateful if you could let me know the position by return.'

In a reply to Mr Johnson dated 10 December, Dr Narain profusely apologized for not having given a specific reply to ONGC since he was not certain of when CSIR would eventually release him. He asked for some more time to get the decision of CSIR President, Indira Gandhi.

Dr Hari Narain must have later met Johnson on a couple of occasions, still, he did not given any acceptance to ONGC's offer nor did he indicate any firm date. Exasperated by Hari Narain's dilly dallying, Johnson finally wrote to Hari Narain on 6 April 1970, asking him to give him, by mid-April, a confirmed joining date. Johnson further wrote that in case he did not receive a firm date, he would have no option but to withdraw the offer, even though he would be personally unhappy. Dr Narain, finally on 28 April, expressed his inability to join ONGC and regretted the inconvenience that he had caused to Johnson and ONGC.

That was certainly, what appears to be, a desperate attempt that lasted nearly 10 months by ONGC and Mr Johnson to get back Dr Narain as Director of RTI.

In retrospect, one would wonder why ONGC and Johnson in particular were so anxious to secure the services of Dr Narain, dangling unusual incentives and 18 advance increments.

Outstanding Academic Career

Dr Narain had had an outstanding academic career. It was at Allahabad University that Narain secured his B.Sc, M.Sc and D.Phil degrees in physics, the latter under the supervision and guidance of Prof. KS Krishnan. Thereafter, he joined Sydney University in Australia where he was awarded a doctorate in geophysics.

After returning to India, Dr Hari Narain joined ONGC as Superintending Geophysicist. His career graph makes for an unusual reading. Perhaps, no other individual has ever occupied or held such high and diverse positions as Dr Narain. He was the Surveyor General of India for four years from 1972 onwards (it was the first time that a non-engineer held this august office); he was also the Vice Chancellor of Banaras University from 1978-81. It is said that Hari Narain was the only vice chancellor of this university during whose tenure no strike took place. As the vice chancellor, he also periodically took classes which the students there happily looked forward to. Later, he was also chief coordinator of a UNDP project. He held many other important assignments and was held in great regard and esteem both by his peers and the government.

Hari Narain was a great scholar. In Australia, he had carried out extensive gravity and magnetic surveys, and his pioneering work in the eastern and central parts of Australia had thrown new light on the tectonics and subsurface geological and crustal structures.

As the Director of NGRI, Dr Hari Narain had established several new research groups like seismology, exploration geophysics, airborne magnetic surveys, geophysical instrumentation, rock mechanics, high-pressure physical properties of rocks and minerals, paleomagnetic laboratory, magnetic observatory, geochemistry, geochronology and geological studies division. He had created an ambience of scientific research at NGRI and seemed to feel at home there. No wonder, he spent much of his working life at that institute.

The awards and honours that came Dr Hari Narain's way are too many to be enumerated in his profile. It would suffice to say that he had won almost every honour and award that was available in his chosen profession.

S Aditya
An Unassuming Geologist

(March 1985–April 1986)

S Aditya was one of the most unassuming and low profile geologists. He was a contemporary of SN Talukdar in the famed Presidency College, Calcutta and had joined ONGC almost at the same time in 1956. Like Talukdar, Aditya too has settled down in Dehra Dun. But unlike him, Aditya is his own man and lives life on his own terms.

Instead of becoming a researcher in the field of geosciences that he had direly desired, Aditya like some of his peers from GSI, joined ONGC in the very first batch of pioneers. He was initially posted as a field geologist in the Kangra foothills in January 1957 and remained in the interior of that area for nearly four years as a member of a field survey party.

His commendable job as a field party member made the bosses take note, and he was sent to Russia for advance training in exploration and oilfield development. That training was one of the most significant turning points in his life. What had really attracted him to the more practical aspects of field geology was the opportunity to know more about reservoir studies. On his return from Russia, Aditya was briefly posted in Ahmedabad. Later, he was sent to Ankleshwar as the resident geologist to work along with a Russian team that was then developing the area.

From the year 1966 to the middle of 1968, he was in Calcutta; he came back to Dehra Dun in July 1968 as the in-charge of production and development in the geology directorate. In October 1970, he was deputed to USA as a UNDP Fellow for petroleum studies. During that excursion, he had acquired enormous knowledge of exploration and field development.

His knowledge in field geology won him accolades, and he was sent to Assam in 1973 as the chief geologist, where he worked for two years. In 1975, the Chairman, NB Prasad sent him to KDMIPE as the head of the prestigious Basin Studies Group (BSG). In March 1985, he was appointed the Director of KDMIPE. He then remained associated with that institute till his superannuation in April 1986. He has several achievements to his credit as the head of Basin Studies Group. He and his team had made a prognostic reserve estimation of all the basins with a Russian team; the BSG team had another collaborative project with the Romanian scientists. He led a team of Indian geoscientists in Abu Dhabi for basin evaluation to study the Arabian country.

He is a voracious reader and reads any book that he gets hold of. But he is also very choosy about what he reads. Among some of the books that have fascinated him are *The White Tiger* by Aravind Adiga and *Sea of Poppies* by Amitav Ghosh. He found *Sea of Poppies* fascinating and intellectually stimulating, even though Adiga's *The White Tiger* had won the Booker Prize.

Surely, if he had not become an exploration scientist, he might have turned a literary critic.

KN Bhave
A Pioneer in Computerization

(September 1986–June 1987)

*K*N *Bhave too belonged to the young group of geoscientists who had joined ONGC in 1956. He has a master's degree in physics from the Agra University.*

During his early years in ONGC, he led gravity-magnetic survey crews in Kutch and Jaisalmer during 1957-1960. After working in a seismic crew in the Ganga Valley in 1960-1961, he was deputed the following year to the USSR and Hungary on a UN fellowship for advanced training in seismic methods.

On his return, he led a seismic reflection crew in Bihar and Gujarat, from 1962–1968. He was selected for six months of intensive training in computer maintenance and programming at Honeywell in 1968. He has had the unique distinction of heading ONGC's first digital computer centre at RTI from 1969–1974.

In 1975, he was appointed to head ONGC's first computerized offshore geophysical survey vessel, *MV Anveshak*. Later, he got training in satellite navigation at Magnavox, USA. He also headed offshore geophysical operations groups of ONGC at Mumbai for seven years; later, he supervised data processing and interpretation work for three years.

In 1985, Bhave was transferred to KDMIPE to head the computer services division from 1985–1987. In 1986–1987, he worked as the Director of KDMIPE. In 1987, he got fully involved in the establishment of the multi-disciplinary data processing, interpretation and evaluation centre GEOPIC at Dehra Dun. Thus he was the first head of the newly formed GEOPIC.

In a way, Bhave was the pioneer of computerization of multi-disciplinary data processing, interpretation and evaluation in ONGC.

Another of his important assignments was as the Regional Director of the central region in Calcutta. He was involved in all phases of geophysical work like live gravity, magnetic, seismic, onshore and offshore data acquisition, processing, evaluation, planning for over 45 years.

During his long stint with ONGC, Bhave visited several countries for technology scouting, selection of equipment, design of survey vessel, data processing, conferences and management training. These countries included USA, the USSR, Germany, Canada, Japan, Norway, Italy, Singapore and so on.

He was life member of the Society of Petroleum Geophysicists, Association of Exploration Geophysicists and Indian Geophysical Union. He received the *Lifetime Achievement Award* from the AEG in 1995.

After his retirement from ONGC in October 1993, he had been engaged in providing consultancy in geophysics to oil exploration companies.

SC Roy Choudhury
A Brilliant Geologist

(June 1987–Mar 1989)

Sarat Chandra Roy Choudhury had had an eventful career in ONGC spanning 35 years. When he retired as Regional Director in 1989, he had virtually mastered almost every phase of ONGC's operations.

He was a brilliant student, having won scholarships both for his B.Sc. and M.Sc. in geology. Later in 1962–63, he did a one-year diploma in hydrocarbon exploration and production from Moscow under a scholarship given by UNDP. Subsequently, in 1984, he also obtained a diploma in business management from IIM, Ahmedabad.

Two of his important assignments were with ONGC's Iraq Project in Basrah. He was Chief of Exploration during 1975–1977 and later General Manager (overseas operations) in 1979–1983. In these capacities, he was instrumental to a large extent in discovering oil in Abu Khema, near Basrah in Iraq.

He served as the Director of the Institute of Reservoir Studies (IRS), Ahmedabad (1983–1987). During his tenure, he was the force behind establishing EOR pilot projects. Besides the institute's activities, he was instrumental in establishing a computer centre (Abacus Centre). To him also goes the credit of constructing a 450-seat capacity auditorium with the facility for simultaneous translation in three languages. As the National Project Director under UNDP (1984–1989), Roy Choudhury was also instrumental in establishing a three-storeyed laboratory and training centre for petroleum and reservoir engineers.

During his tenure with ONGC, Roy Choudhury was elected the Vice President of World Petroleum Congress held in Houston (1987). He was also elected Chairman of the Ahmedabad chapter of the Society of Petroleum Engineers (SPE) in 1986–1987 as also of its Dehra Dun chapter in 1987–1989.

After his superannuation from ONGC, he had been actively involved with numerous projects in private and public sectors. He is the author of over 15 papers in the E & P sectors which have been published in national and international journals.

Dr SK Biswas
Man With a Vision

(May 1989–June 1993)

*D*r *SK Biswas was among the 130 odd geoscientists and others who were in the first and the only batch to have joined ONGC in 1956. He had done his master's in geology from Calcutta University. Later in 1978, Biswas obtained a doctorate in science.*

During his career, spanning 38 years, he had rendered distinguished service to ONGC in various positions.

He superannuated from ONGC in June 1993 as the Director of KDMIPE.

During his career in ONGC, Biswas was given several foreign assignments that included consultations, technical co-operation and collaborations, negotiations and participation in conferences, seminars. symposiums and meetings.

He performed all these challenging assignments with much credit and acquired more than three decades of

hands-on, in-field, online and offline operational, R & D and management experience in all facets of the upstream petroleum industry. His contributions in all these fields were of great national and global significance. For a decade and half, Biswas had been at the leading edge of all R & D related activities of the Indian petroleum exploration industry. During the last five years of his career, he was among the top scientists who were given the responsibility to reengineer the vision, set the goals, formulate the strategies, restructure the plan and effectively implement and manage the programmes of all important operational and R & D activities related to the exploration.

His role as the General Manager (exploration) of Bombay Regional Business Centre during 1986–1989 was considered to be of great significance. He is recognized as an authority on the geology of Indian sedimentary basins on which he has several publications to his credit.

Biswas had done many training and professional courses in India and abroad during his long career with ONGC. Even though he had retired from ONGC, his passion for his profession continues to remain unabated. Because of that, he has been actively involved in several organizations both as a consultant and advisor. He is also the member of various core committees in government departments.

Dr Biswas was the recipient of several honours including *L Rama Rao Award* from the GSI and the *National Mineral Award*.

He has several publications to his credit. Over a 100 of his papers were published in national and international journals.

Kuldeep Chandra
A Multifaceted Scientist

(July 1993–July 2001)

With a master's degree in physical chemistry from the famed Lucknow University, Kuldeep Chandra joined ONGC at a relatively young age of 19. To him goes the credit of being the Founder Member of the geochemistry laboratories at KDMIPE.

Soon enough, he got the opportunity to join the French Institute of Petroleum where he expanded his horizon in all the facets of geochemistry during his eight months' training.

In the course of his tenure at ONGC spanning 39 years, Chandra has had the opportunity of working at various work centres; he introduced state of the art geochemical methodologies and groomed a large number of scientists who were later able to cater to the voluminous requirement of geochemical data acquisition, both at the institute and in the network of regional exploration labs in Baroda, Bombay, Madras and Sibsagar.

Chandra had the unique distinction of leading geochemical field parties in almost all the sedimentary basins in the country that conducted geochemical surveys. He made an assessment of oil occurrence in Bombay High.

His contribution towards development of original methodologies in geochemistry of source rock, geochemical surveys, and genetic classification of oils, natural gases and oil field waters is still talked about. He was also instrumental in making the first volumetric genetic estimates of hydrocarbons in the Cambay and Kaveri basins.

Chandra also helped setting up an edifice of the quantitative 3D genetic basin modelling, which led to the development of integrated synergic exploration systems. He is a recipient of prestigious *National Mineral Award* (1989) for his contribution to geochemistry and for development of integrated petroleum exploration systems.

As second in command in the Exploration Business Group in the southern region (1985–1988), he contributed towards the enhancement of the quality of drilling fluid and oil well cementation jobs. During his tenure at Madras, he also prepared a guide book for drilling fluid engineers to ensure cost-effective drilling operations.

Predictive Source-Rock Modelling

In southern region, Chandra developed a predictive source-rock modelling based on the relationship between the sea level changes and source potential. This work became an integral part of a special publication by American Association of Petroleum Geologists (AAPG) on source rocks in sequence stratigraphic framework.

Chandra led a team of the Geosciences Research Group of KDMIPE during 1988–1991. His leadership greatly contributed to the preparation of ONGC's eighth plan for R & D, Accelerated Programme of Exploration (APEX), National Seismic Programme (NSP) and Joint Venture Exploration Block Identification.

Chandra was also the Director of Institute of Management Development during 1991–1993 and introduced organizational development programmes through work climate surveys followed by interactional management development workshops. These programmes helped groom responsible and responsive executives.

As Director of KDMIPE, Chandra greatly contributed to the growth and quality enhancement of integrated geosciences research, basin studies and exploration economics. Under his leadership, the state of the art technologies have been absorbed and developed. He had provided the thrust to a generation of over 400 exploratory locations.

25-Year Perspective Plan

Chandra's team at KDMIPE had also prepared a comprehensive 25-year (2000–2025) Perspective Plan for exploration based on a fresh assessment of hydrocarbon resources of Indian sedimentary basins and perspectives for overseas exploration. He had organized back-up to OVL for evaluation of proposals for overseas exploration opportunities.

One of his other contributions was the launching of ONGC Institutes' Integrated Services (OIIS). That was an initiative to provide revenue generating services to various operators in the upstream sector in order to make productive use of facilities available in the new environment of liberalization. Thus, the various ONGC's institutes could generate revenue of about 10 per cent of their annual budget.

Chandra is an expert faculty for varied subjects with the management development institutions of the oil sector. Many of his colleagues have obtained a doctorate of philosophy in science under his able guidance. He was invited by OAPEC in 1982 to hold a seminar on petroleum geochemistry for the exploration managers of Arabian countries.

The Indian Geophysical Union in 1996 conferred the Decennial Gold Medal to Chandra for his lifelong services to petroleum exploration in India.

Chandra is member of a number of professional national and international societies including GSI, Indian Council of Chemists, Indian Society of Mass Spectrometry and Indian Society of Phytochemistry and Economic Botany, and Society of Applied Geochemistry.

Chandra was also one of the architects of PETROTECH Conference and successfully organized Petrotech-95 and Petrotech-97.

Post retirement, Chandra has continued his academic pursuits both as a consultant and faculty. He is very actively involved in conducting courses and preparing project reports at the University of Petroleum and Energy Studies (UPES).

Dr Debabrata Ray
A Specialist in PSCs

(August 2001–April 2005)

Dr Debabrata Ray became head of KDMIPE in October 2001. His four-year long tenure was noteworthy for several achievements.

He had joined ONGC in 1967 as an assistant geologist after obtaining a master's degree in applied geology from IIT Kharagpur. Later in 1982, he earned his doctorate in geology from MS University, Baroda.

For over three decades, Dr Ray was closely engaged in exploration and development geology in various sedimentary basins, specializing in synergic interpretation of geoscientific data. The data thus accumulated, helped formulate exploration plans and strategies; it also greatly helped in the management of the production sharing contracts as also joint venture exploration and development programmes in India.

During his tenure at KDMIPE, he was intimately associated with multi-disciplinary studies for understanding the petroleum geology and hydrocarbon habitat of several basins of India, particularly the Bengal and KG basins. During his earlier years in ONGC, he had worked at this institute for seven years during 1975 to 1982, as a geologist.

He was also the head of EXCOM Group from 1997 to 2001. It was a challenging assignment especially in view of the opening up of upstream petroleum sectors in the 90s.

However, it goes to his credit that he had successfully met that challenge. The job involved negotiating several

Production Sharing Contracts (PSC) and other related agreements on behalf of ONGC with the government as also Indian and multinational companies. He also negotiated production sharing contracts pertaining to acquisition of foreign E & P acreages by OVL.

As the working group coordinator, he had handled the entire gamut of activities for submission of global bids on behalf of ONGC and OVL for purchase of equity in foreign companies. He also coordinated ONGC's strategic alliances with multinational E & P companies for deep water exploration and exploitation in the country.

Dr Ray was a member of the sub-group for India Hydrocarbon Vision-2020 on 'Restructuring and Disinvestment' and associated with its work for India Hydrocarbon Vision-2025 on 'Strategy for Exploration and Production Covering Technology and Environmental Issues'.

Dr Ray has co-chaired the Business Interactive Group Session of the SPG International Conference in Madras (1998) and the Exploration in Frontier Areas of SPG International Conference in New Delhi (2000).

His paper on *Production Sharing Contracts and Joint Venture Exploration and Development Programmes in India*, presented at a conference in Singapore in 1996, was greatly appreciated. As an invited speaker, he had presented a paper on *Petroleum E&P Activities into the New Millennium—The Indian Scenario* at the International Conference in Malaysia. Dr Ray got recognition for his professional excellence in October 2000, when he chaired the Oral and Poster Sessions of 'Petroleum Systems of India' during the AAPG and Indonesian Petroleum Association International Conference and Exhibitions, held at Bali, Indonesia.

PB Pati
The Shortest Tenure

(April 2005–May 2005)

PB Pati was KDMIPE head barely for 37 days before he retired. This was indeed the shortest tenure of a KDMIPE director. He had obtained a master's degree in applied geology from IIT Kharagpur in 1967 and joined ONGC the same year.

His career in ONGC began as a well site geologist in the Cambay and Assam basins. He was closely associated with the exploration and development geology in various sedimentary basins, especially the Cambay and Mumbai Offshore basins. His specialty however was in Cambay Basin.

Dr DM Kale
A Reservoir Specialist

(May 2005–April 2006)

*W*ith a doctorate in astrophysics from the prestigious Tata Institute of Fundamental Research, Dr Dilip M Kale joined ONGC. Very soon, he had become one of the recognized specialists in reservoir management.

His first job in ONGC was to develop Numerical Reservoir Simulators; as a talented scientist, he conceptualized several projects for Enhanced Oil Recovery (EOR). He was also the head of the Exploration Business Groups at different times in Eastern and Mumbai regions.

One of his noteworthy achievements was to establish a computerized simulation at the Institute of Reservoir Studies (IRS), Ahmedabad.

He was Head, KDMIPE for one year in 2005-06. It was due to his initiative that Underground Coal Gasification (UCG) activity was restarted in 2005. During his tenure as Head of COIN, Dr Kale coordinated all the research and development activities at the various research institutes of ONGC. On 1 August 2008, he took over as Director General of ONGC Energy Centre at Delhi. It was again due to his initiative that ONGC set up a dedicated Energy Centre for research, development and demonstration of all alternate sources of energy.

Amongst the numerous awards that he had won, the most noteworthy was the *Peter the Great* presented by the Russian Academy of Natural Sciences.

He also published a number of technical papers in national and international journals.

Jokhan Ram
Acclaimed Keynote Speaker

(April 2006–January 2008)

Jokhan Ram came to ONGC with a gold medal in geology from the Banaras Hindu University.

During his 38-year stint with ONGC, he was greatly involved in exploration and development geology in various sedimentary basins in different capacities.

His main areas of interest included well site geological work, field geological mapping, remote sensing, integrated basin analysis, structural geomorphology, seismic interpretation and exploration management.

One of his most significant contributions was in preparing the Sedimentary Basins Map of India that is now being marketed by KDMIPE. He is also the co-author of regional geological map of the Himalayan foothills.

Ram also led an ONGC team in some prestigious collaboration projects such as the Indo-Soviet collaborative project on geological prospects and recommendations for future exploration, and deep drilling under high pressure in the Himalayan foothills.

He contributed more than 36 technical papers on varied themes that were published in national and international journals. He had been associated in various capacities with a number of research institutes, universities and government entities. Additionally, he was an acclaimed keynote speaker and had chaired several technical sessions at various national and international conferences and symposia.

PK Bhowmick

Though most people aspire to reach the top step of their respective hierarchical ladder, very few really deserve it and, worse still, have the requisite will power to succeed. Among these few deserving individuals is Pradut Kumar Bhowmick.

As the 19th Executive Director and Head of KDMIPE, Bhowmick has seen and done it all. He boasts of a first class master's degree in applied geology from the University of Delhi. Before he joined ONGC in 1976 as a graduate trainee, Bhowmick had done some teaching in the Delhi College of Engineering and also worked as a mining geologist with Rajasthan State Mines and Minerals Corporation. He has had an illustrious career spanning more than 35 years; early in his career, he has had the unique distinction of having worked in various sedimentary basins that included Cambay, Assam, Arakan, Krishna-Godavari and Mumbai Offshore. Additionally, he also worked in some of the overseas basins.

His first job as a well site geologist in ONGC was a great learning experience. He was attached to the operational geology group in Mumbai, and during those five years, Bhowmick learnt the nitty-gritty of his profession.

Exceptional Talent

This experience came in very handy when he was posted to KDMIPE in 1982; there he learnt the ropes of an exploration and development geologist. For the following six years, he worked with utmost dedication. At KDMIPE, he along with his team developed an exploration model and play concept for the *Early to Middle Eocene Sands*; this eventually led to the discovery of Bechraji field in the northern and eastern extension of Jatana field; it also helped in the identification of future areas for exploration. One of his assignments was with the Reservoir Modelling Group where he developed geological models for reservoir modelling.

In Nazira, Assam, Bhowmick was attached to the Exploration and Development Group and there too, he showed an exceptional talent. Chennai was his next stop in 1991, where again, he was associated with the Exploration and Development Group. His posting on deputation in the Directorate General of Hydrocarbons (DGH) from 1994–1998 gave him ample opportunities in enlarging his professional canvas.

He further enriched his experience when he was posted in the Exploration and Development Directorate in Dehra Dun in 1998 and later in Western Offshore Basin in Mumbai. He returned to Dehra Dun in 2007 and was elevated as Head of KDMIPE on 1 February 2008. It was here that his vast experience came to the fore when he gave a remarkable makeover to India's premier R & D institute, and a jewel in the ONGC's crown. During the past three years and more, the performance of this institute has shown excellent results. It was under Bhowmick's stewardship that the first shale gas project in India was undertaken. Other major achievements during Bhowmick's tenure were: sequence stratigraphy, water shut off job for GNPOC in Sudan, structural modelling, and basin marketing.

Virtual Reality Centre

One of the most important jobs was setting up of a state of the art Virtual Reality Centre (VRC) that catered to the scientists of different disciplines engaged in oil exploration. He had also encouraged acceleration in research activities, and as a result KDMIPE had already applied for two patents, one of which is on geomicrobiological prospecting.

'All work and no play make Jack a dull boy.' Keeping that adage in mind, Bhowmick started a well equipped gymnasium for the institute's staffers.

He is highly computer savvy and has been instrumental in designing a new reporting system for the oil and gas reserves in ONGC in Oracle, and is familiar with the workstation environment of interpreting seismic data.

Bhowmick had been an active member of the American Association of Petroleum Geologists since 1978, and is also a member of SPG and APG, and has quite a few papers to his credit.

SV Rao

*S*V Rao was the 13th Director (exploration) of
ONGC. He was elevated to this position on
25 February 2011.

Rao has had a distinguished career
spanning over three and a half
decades. His wide ranging experience
in exploration and exploitation
of oil and gas fields covers the
entire gamut of exploration, well
site investigations, geological and
geophysical assessment. Rao was
also the head of two of the most critical basins of ONGC,
namely, Krishna-Godavari and Western Offshore. He was also
involved with deep water operations.

One of his key postings was as the Head of the Exploration
and Development Directorate, Dehra Dun, a corporate
exploration wing of ONGC. Its work was considered vital,
and even some geoscientists called it 'eyes and ears of
director (exploration)'. He was a no-nonsense man and
didn't tolerate fools.

CHAPTER 18

Epilogue

ONGC: History and Me

RAJ KANWAR

In what way did the writing of ONGC's history change me? And in what ways did the very act of writing this book bring about a metamorphosis in my daily routine?

I have oftentimes asked myself these questions since June 30 2005—the day I submitted the completed manuscript.

There are no simple, black and white answers. Like any other endeavour in life, this experience too came in variegated hues, even shades of grey. Yet, it was not like anything else that I had experienced before in my chequered life, stretching over 75 summers, and 75 winters, and identical number of autumns and springs. Yes, a man's life has all of these seasons, many ups and many downs, *kabhi dhoop, kabhi chhaon*.

I retired as the Chairman of SK Oilfield Equipment Company Pvt Ltd on 8 October 2000; that day I had turned 70, having led a very hectic, fulfilled and satisfying life. I relinquished that position not because I had felt tired or jaded; far from that. In fact, my mind had become much sharper, my reflexes quicker and my business acumen got further honed. I had been in business for nearly 30 years, and thought that enough was enough. The company was in good health, and in the capable hands of my older son, Manav.

Uttarakhand Agitation

I longed to resume my literary pursuits, to write columns for mainstream dailies, and to write biographies. The national dailies said, "No, thank you. We are already choc-a-block with columnists. However, the *Himachal Times* of Dehra Dun heartily welcomed me; in my daily column *'A View From the Balcony'* in which I wrote on every facet of the then ongoing agitation for the creation of a separate state of Uttarakhand. There was much appreciation, but it wasn't the real thing; I gave that up. Then, the weekly *Garhwal Post* took me on board, and my column *'Frankly Speaking'* became a big hit. But those columns did not give me the inner satisfaction; I yearned to reach a larger readership, with something of literary value.

Raj Kanwar and Satish Sharma of *Garhwal Post* with Subir Raha

My friend of 50 years, Ruskin Bond, readily agreed to the idea of me writing his biography. I was again enthused, and managed to complete in no time four chapters about his early years. Simultaneously, I started working on another book tentatively titled *Women of Substance*, that would carry the biographies of eight famous living Indian women. Two of them promptly consented.

In fact, I had just then started working on those two books when Subir Raha invited me to write the history of ONGC that would synchronize with the commencement of its Golden Jubilee celebrations. The *Women of Substance* was then put on a back-burner.

Two Editorial Associates

The invitation that came in September 2004 had December 15 as the deadline for the submission of the first draft, less than three months away. I sincerely believed that ONGC did not mean it. But no, ONGC was dead serious, and Dr Ashok Balyan more so. Fortunately, ONGC provided me with two editorial associates. Shobha Singh, a geologist from Mumbai, and Aniruddha Pattnaik, a 14-day off-and-on driller from *Sagar Vijay*, joined me; they turned out to be both talented and enthusiastic. But they were not full-time. Initially, Pattnaik worked on his off days from his home base in Kolkatta, and Shobha worked in Mumbai, tracking retired ONGCians, as the two continued to perform their respective official duties. In the later stages, I could manage to get them to Dehra Dun for some time, and that helped a lot.

The Preface has explained, at length, the nuts and bolts of writing the history of ONGC. I will only narrate in this piece how the process of writing the book personally affected me in so many ways that I couldn't have imagined was possible. Let me explain.

After my retirement, I was a free bird, and led a carefree life. My daily column, 1,000–1,200 words in length, took two hours in gathering inputs, and another couple of hours in writing. The weekly column was much more difficult an assignment as it required choosing week after week a topical yet interesting subject. Thus my attention span in those days of column writing was barely two hours; and it was easy to stay focused. I also read a lot; four English dailies, three or four magazines, and whatever books took my fancy. Some musts on my daily schedule then were an hour's walk in the morning, siesta in the afternoon and an 8 pm date with two whiskies.

That ONGC history assignment had upset much of my daily routine; the morning walk went for a toss; sometimes I wrote till three in the morning, and on other occasions, I began my day at three; whiskey did not remain a daily ritual, and siesta too became irregular. For days on, some of the newspapers remained unopened. In some ways, all of that came as a real blessing, since I realized that every habit, even a good one, is a bad habit. In a way, it was good riddance. We also shunned socializing, stopped visiting the Doon Club; *Diwali* in 2004 was a low-key affair. Also, our annual visit to the US was put in abeyance, despite entreaties from our granddaughter to attend her graduation ceremony.

My Gains Were Many

However, I gained much more than what I had lost by way of missed opportunities. My attention span doubled to four hours; thus I was able to put my writing, rewriting and editing schedule in a four-hour time span. At 75, it becomes difficult to stay focused for any length of time. One's mind oscillates playfully towards temptations and distractions—such are the wages of old age. That I could stay focused that long was a pleasant realization. My thought process too, showed greater clarity, and I could visualize much farther than before. All that helped me map, at the outset, the entire chapter. The pace of my writing picked up; also at places, it assumed lyrical tones. Equally important, my editing became natural and easy, untouched by any laboured process; editing was simply a matter of reflex action.

During my years in professional journalism, I invariably did better against a shorter deadline. That experience came in handy when I started writing the narrative history against a deadline that constantly loomed large over my head like the Sword of Damocles. Then suddenly I realized that Dr Balyan's sacrosanct deadline was turning out to be a blessing in disguise. A comfortable deadline would have lulled me into lethargy, with disastrous consequences.

Recalling my university days, I remembered that I always scored higher marks in end-to-end examination papers but did not fare so well, if there was a big gap between two papers. Having said this, it must be remembered that every creative and productive endeavour has a minimal time frame, and a shorter period would tell on its quality.

Let me illustrate. An expectant mother asked her four-year-old son what present he would like for his birthday. 'Mummy, I want a little baby sister.' Aghast, the mother said, 'Your birthday is only a month away, Papa is only one man, he can't produce the baby girl so fast.' Undaunted, the little boy suggested, 'Oh; Mom, why don't you put more men on the job?' Apocryphal, the story might be, but its moral is that there are certain jobs that can't be done quickly without compromising.

But the more perceptible change that came was in my attitude towards people close to me, and my perception of them was truly amazing. My conversations became more circumspect; I started thinking before speaking; I began weighing my words for their consequences. I stopped making instant judgements since I realized I have no right to judge other peoples' actions.

Happily, I lost, for good, my short temper. If I saw my fuse was about to blow, I would take two deep breaths; and that helped. All of these self-improvements came because I started putting myself in other person's shoes. That was a big help.

A Day of Heartbreak

On 14 August 2006, a day that should have been my happiest day in a long time, turned out to be my saddest. That was the momentous day when the then Union Petroleum Minister, Murli Deora, had formally released *Upstream India* at an impressive function in Dehra Dun. I had waited anxiously for that event for one year. Neither the emcee nor anyone else announced my name, when the book was released, as if I had suddenly become a *persona non grata*. A Libran is very emotional, and an old Libran is more so. That was a moment of heartbreak. I am normally very prone to shedding tears; even a small display of emotions or sentiments in a Hindi movie would make me cry (that's why I don't watch movies). My guardian angel, luckily, saved me from embarrassment, for somehow I controlled my tears. Fortunately, my wife sat in the front row with Col Wahi and others, and I in a back row, otherwise she would have guessed my emotional turbulence.

I felt certain that the lapse in the protocol that day couldn't have been intentional; just an inadvertent omission. I slunk away when the function ended, not even caring to stay for the lunch to which, in any case, I was not invited.

.....and Then Came the Thank You Dinner

That the *faux pas* was absolutely unintended was doubly confirmed when CMD, RS Sharma, himself invited me at a special 'Thank You' dinner on 9 October at the Taj Mansingh Hotel in New Delhi. Also invited were all the ONGC veterans whom I had interviewed during the course of writing the book as also others connected with the history project. Both Dr Balyan and M Rajagopala Rao made laudatory references to my effort and my contribution in their introductory speeches. I was also invited to speak.

That was the night I was in seventh heaven, in a manner of speaking. Both my wife and my older son must have felt very proud of me. There is nothing more satisfying and rewarding for a 76-year-old man to see a glint of pride in his son's eyes and an unspoken and unsaid praise from his wife of 41 years. If 14 August was a day of heartbreak, the night of 9 October brought me immense joy and satisfaction. In fact, that was one of the most rewarding nights of my eventful and long professional and business career.

The 'Thank you' dinner on Monday, 9 October was a memorable event for most of us. ONGC's hospitality was lavish. Many of the veterans, who had come from various parts of the country, were overwhelmed. 'We didn't expect ONGC to send us business class return air tickets, but they did. And then we were put up in the best of the hotels in Delhi, and each one of us had a taxi at his disposal in Delhi. The dinner was fabulous. We have never before received such generous hospitality', said a veteran from Mumbai. Another praised CMD RS Sharma for remembering the old veterans, and for showering on them generous hospitality. 'We now truly feel an inalienable part of the larger ONGC *parivaar,*' he further added.

What Does History Mean to ONGC?

ONGC's history is a story of selfless people, some ordinary, some not-so ordinary and some extraordinary, who deservedly earned the sobriquet of pioneers. It was such people who blazed new trails in those early years of its inception. All of them left their footprints on the sands of time, and stories of their dare devilry needed to be told and retold so that the successive generations that follow in their footsteps, could draw inspiration. Thus the history of ONGC is one such story that deserved to be recorded for posterity.

And finally, how did I get involved in the writing of ONGC's history? There must have been many far more qualified people in the country, even in ONGC, for this task. Then why did the then CMD of ONGC, Subir Raha pick me?—A retired journalist, a retired businessman—yes retired, but not tired. Raha didn't even know me when he joined ONGC in May 2001. He was just two months into his job, when I interviewed him on two or three occasions for *Garhwal Post*. Maybe, something in those interviews caught his eyes or tickled his sharp mind. Or perhaps he wanted someone who has a special feel for ONGC—someone who is an insider, and yet without any baggage of the insider—someone who could at the same time be objective, unbiased and frank. My formal association with ONGC as its PRO had lasted just three years. Yet, I remained associated with this organization and hundreds of ONGCians at various levels for 50 years or so. But all of that was not known to Raha; yet his choice fell on me.

To Raha goes the prime credit of having the history of ONGC written. But for his vision and farsightedness, the history project wouldn't have come to fruition. This and other books, will stand testimony to Raha's out-of-the-box thinking, and together with the ONGC Museum, will be his legacy to the nation.

I have done an honest job to the best of my ability working eight to 10 hours daily. For me, it was a professional challenge that I dared accept in my twilight years. My two associates, Pattnaik and Shobha Singh, were wonderful. The two of them learnt as much from this venture as I did. Learning is a lifelong process, and I must confess that I learnt a lot from this experience, and became much, much richer in the process.

Thanks to ONGC, and the rare opportunity I got of writing its history, I now feel more confident in resuming the two major biographical projects I had put on a back-burner. That is what the writing of ONGC's history has meant to me; it has given me a much greater degree of confidence and self-assurance. In fact, the writing of the history has restored my own faith in my ability to undertake even bigger writing projects.

Strange though it may seem, ONGC, in one way or another, has always been involved in numerous milestones that I passed by in my life.

My association with ONGC—covering a period of over 60 years—impacted my life in many, many ways. It would take me 50,000 or more words if I were to narrate my very unique relationship with ONGC and, by extension, with hundreds of ONGCians. God willing, I will write all about those 50 years on another occasion, at another time.

I now seek the hospitality of ONGC Reports to express my sincerest thanks to CMD RS Sharma, and Director (HR), Dr AK Balyan for the singular recognition that they and ONGC accorded me and to the score of veteran ONGCians on the night of 9 October 2006—a night that will always stay in my memory as long as I live.